A TERRIER GOES TO WAR

J. Roberts

MINERVA PRESS

ATLANTA LONDON SYDNEY

A TERRIER GOES TO WAR
Copyright © J. Roberts 1998

All Rights Reserved

ISBN 0 75410 257 2

First Published 1998 by
MINERVA PRESS
Sixth Floor
Canberra House
315–317 Regent Street
London W1R 7YB

Printed in Great Britain for Minerva Press

A TERRIER GOES TO WAR

*To the members of the Red Cross organisation
who will never know how much we prisoners appreciated their
parcels. Without a doubt they made the difference between life
and death for many of us, as well as confirming that we were
not forgotten by those back home.
Thank you, Red Cross.*

About the Author

The Author was born in February 1919 in Chelsea, London and was the youngest of five children. Following the War he worked for BOAC. He retired early from being an accountant for British Airways and has lived in Devon for the past twenty years with wife, Diana.

To my wife Diana
without whose encouragement, nagging and love,
this book would never have been written

Preface

This is a true story of the experience of a member of the Territorial Army (or 'Terrier') from the time of the Munich crisis in September 1938 until demobilisation in February 1946. The names of some of the characters have been slightly altered in case they do not wish to be identified but they will easily recognise themselves.

Obviously in the Army, and particularly in a prison camp, swearing constitutes a large part of a soldier's normal language but I have omitted swearing from this story and have decided to leave it to the reader's imagination. There may however be one or two instances where I have had to include swearing otherwise the full impact of the instances would be lost.

Chapter 1

From Munich to War

I was nineteen years old and sitting in the John Lewis canteen with Eric Bagley, Billy Parker and several others having a meal one September afternoon in 1938 and of course the main topic of conversation was Neville Chamberlain's much publicised visit to Munich and his so-called triumphant return waving a piece of paper. Most of us thought that in spite of the publicity and paper waving it was only a respite and that war was inevitable before very long.

Eric said 'My brother Alec has joined the Queen Victoria Rifles which is part of the Territorial Army; why don't we all go and join?'

This led to a long discussion, after which we all agreed to go to the Drill Hall in Davies Street that evening to enlist in the Territorial Army. About seven o'clock that evening we met in the Pub in Oxford Street and after a few drinks we went to the Drill Hall and following the completion of our enlistment forms we duly became the John Lewis Platoon in the First Battalion of the Queen Victoria Rifles.

It then became an established practice for us to meet in the pub at least once a week before going to the Drill Hall for training.

I could never decide whether it was the drinking session in the Pub or the training that was the main attraction, but they were always well attended and in due course we were issued with uniforms but because of a shortage we had to share rifles.

The Powers that be decided that the Queen Victoria Rifles should become the first motorcycle regiment in the British Army and in the early summer of 1939 the battalion was issued with civilian motorcycles of both solo and sidecar types and from then on our training consisted mainly of driving lessons.

On a Friday evening in July at about ten o'clock we met at the Drill Hall and eventually when some semblance of order was achieved we started off in convoy for Tidworth Barracks in Wiltshire for our annual summer training camp.

It was a long convoy consisting of mainly BSA, Norton and Triumph motorcycles with a few Bedford 30 cwt trucks. Because it was at the end of a working week and late at night we were finding it so tiring that it became very difficult to stay awake and to keep our concentration while driving along strange roads. Suddenly one of the motorcycle sidecars shot across the road and jammed into the front entrance of a public house.

'Its that stupid bugger, Nobby Clark, he never could remember opening times,' said Eric.

Fortunately there were no serious injuries although Nobby Clark did have a broken leg and the sidecar passenger had some bruising but certainly the front of the Public House looked the worse for wear.

We eventually arrived at Tidworth Barracks without any further mishaps and settled into the barrack rooms. Then we spent Saturday afternoon and all day Sunday listening to lectures on the role of a motorcycle battalion in particular. Monday saw the beginning of a full but pleasant fortnight spent mainly in weapon training and on the firing ranges trying to hit the targets with a rifle or Bren gun.

After this enjoyable break we returned to our normal workaday life in John Lewis's and to our training sessions at the Drill Hall where we were now concentrating on map-reading exercises and learning to dismantle a Bren gun in a few seconds and to clear any jamming that may occur.

This uneventful life continued until the afternoon of 1st September when the news of the order for general mobilisation spread like wildfire through the John Lewis store in Oxford Street and we heard that all members of the Territorial Army had to report to their Headquarters as soon as possible.

All members of the John Lewis Platoon agreed to meet in the usual Public House at seven o'clock and I went off to my home in Chelsea where I had some tea and spent time allaying my mother's fears before changing into uniform and then dashing over to my girlfriend's house in Battersea to let her know what was happening and to tell her that as soon as I knew exactly where I would be and what I would be doing I would let her know.

I arrived at the public house just after seven o'clock and joined the others in the saloon bar where we sat drinking. About every hour one of us would go round the corner to check on what was happening in the Drill Hall. Nothing occurred that was important enough to make us cut short our drinking so we continued until we got turned out at closing time.

Then we staggered round the corner to the Drill Hall to report officially and after a period of chaos and confusion we were marched (stumbling) along Oxford Street until we turned off and arrived at an empty shop in Wimpole Street and were told to make ourselves at home as this would be our billet for the time being.

In the upstairs rooms we found mattresses spread out on the floor and we all collapsed on to the nearest one, and the next day was spent settling in to our new home. After having breakfast in a canteen behind Selfridges on Sunday morning we were lined up and told that our duties were to be on standby in readiness to help the Police prevent any panic or even rioting by the public, and in view of this task it seemed very convenient that the Wimpole Street shop backed on to the Marylebone Lane Police Station.

A Bedford truck arrived and we were told to climb aboard and were taken to Hyde Park where we were put to work filling sandbags and loading them on to the truck. While we were filling the sandbags we listened to the radio and we heard the Declaration of War and were told to return to our billets immediately.

Shortly after our arrival back at Wimpole Street the air raid warning sounded and we had to go to Baker Street railway station and were ordered to clear all passengers from the platforms and away from the station. Although the people were looking very worried there were no problems and everyone left quietly. After about ten minutes the all clear siren sounded and we then returned to Wimpole Street.

We finished building a barrier of sandbags along the front of the building we were using as billets and then settled down to a rather monotonous existence that generally consisted of going to a canteen behind Selfridges for our meals, running and drilling in Hyde Park, driving lessons and practice on solo and combination motorcycles and trucks in Regent's Park map-reading and weapon training in the Drill Hall in Davies Street and of course an occasional guard duty in front of the Wimpole Street building.

The regulations concerning a strict blackout came into operation which created an eerie atmosphere as well as a lot of confusion in the West End. It caused several minor accidents. I never really became accustomed to it. We were under strict orders not to go outside of a three-block area around the billet, but since to begin with, most of the chaps spent the evenings in the billet the orders did not affect their lives too much.

Gradually more of us became so frustrated with the strict regime that occasionally we ignored the orders and went home. In my case as well as going to Chelsea to see my mother, I also went to Battersea to visit my girlfriend Lilian who lived in a side street composed of small terrace houses behind Battersea Park.

I remember that on numerous occasions we got a lot of pleasure through listening to a young pianist practising his jazz music in a nearby house, and we never realised at the time that he was destined to become one of the greatest jazz musicians of all time. There were also some evenings when members of the original John Lewis Platoon would meet at the public house in Oxford Street and have a few drinks and a good old singsong. Sometimes a few of the chaps would visit the clubs in Soho but although I was no angel this never appealed to me because I would rather spend the evening with my girlfriend. But to be honest probably the most important reason was because I was too mean to spend my money in those sort of places.

Units of the British Army were being sent to France and there was, of course, great speculation as to when we would be going. Being so young and naive at that time we were all looking forward to what we thought would be a great adventure. Our life in the West End continued in the same monotonous routine for about two months and we had no further air raid warnings or any reasons to provide back-up help for the Police. On reflection I think the strangest aspect of our stay in the West End was the sudden transition from a busy metropolis ablaze with lights, neon advertisements, traffic lights with traffic (particularly buses with lights full on) to an almost pitch-black world only lit by shielded dim car lights or small torches carried by pedestrians, inevitably there were many collisions both involving traffic and pedestrians.

It was really remarkable how quickly most people managed to adapt to this strange eerie world of darkness which had appeared almost overnight, and for the most part people reacted in a good-humoured way to any small setbacks.

We were by now becoming quite expert with rifles and machine guns and with all aspects of driving, although most of our motorcycles and trucks were still of a civilian type and not military largely because the country had been so unprepared for war that military equipment had not been manufactured. In fact our rifles were Lee Enfields of 1914 vintage and we were still having to share them, but in spite of all these disadvantages we still thought that we could just go to France and if Germany tried anything we would be able to stop them without any great difficulty.

I believe that my mother and all the other parents were anticipating another Great War with long drawn-out trench warfare and massive casualties, so naturally they were very apprehensive and were worrying far more than their naive sons although of course we *did* wonder what the future had in store for us and we were rather nervous but strangely at the same time full of confidence. I never thought at the time that I would one day look back on this episode in the West End with nostalgia and affection or that there would be many occasions when I would wish that we were back on standby in Wimpole Street, even if it *was* boring and monotonous.

Chapter 2
Garden of Kent to Hell

In November we moved to a Whitbread hop farm called Beltring which was in beautiful countryside just outside the village of Paddock Wood in Kent which, in my opinion, is rightly called the Garden of England.

We were told our billets would be in the large oast houses and of course we would be sleeping on straw mattresses on the floor. It took us very little time to settle in and we then started the usual monotonous round of drilling, weapon training map reading and driving but I also began a course of training to become a wireless operator which involved learning the Morse code, tapping out messages on the key and radio techniques and language.

The weather deteriorated very quickly and soon there was snow and ice everywhere. The water supply was frozen and we had problems getting water to shave with while any other washing was done very quickly, usually in cold water. Since we only had outside latrines, many gladly suffered constipation and our life was fast becoming so miserable that we longed for the comforts of our West End billets and regretted the day we had to leave there.

Gradually the battalion was being brought up to strength by the arrival of men who had been called up for National Service, and we also received brand new Norton motorcycles (solo and combinations), Humber Snipe radio trucks, Bedford 30 cwt. trucks and Daimler armoured scout cars.

We now began spending most of our time on manoeuvres all round Kent and one of the most important parts of our training was how to deal with any landings by paratroopers. The weather was improving all the time and we were thoroughly enjoying our jaunts round the beautiful countryside. I thought it was rather surprising that the rendezvous points invariably turned out to be in close proximity to public houses in quiet villages.

I was now on a Humber Snipe wireless truck with Roger Murray (one of the National Service intake) and we got on very well together. All the new trucks had been fitted with governors to prevent them being driven at more than 50 mph but fortunately one of the chaps was an expert mechanic and he rendered all the governors useless so that we frequently went at 80 mph.

Sadly all good things must come to an end and they did when we were given a course of injections and sent home for a weeks embarkation leave. Shortly after our return from this leave we were ordered to vacate the hop farm and move to various farms in the Ashford area of Kent. Naturally rumours of our ultimate destination included practically every country in the world and the equipment seen arriving at or that had been seen in the quartermaster's store, ranged from pith helmets and Bermuda shorts to snowshoes and skis.

On the farms we slept wherever a space could be found – mostly in barns and outbuildings – but Roger and I decided to make ourselves as comfortable as we could in the wireless truck. It was a very primitive existence with a few outside water taps and latrines.

We were under very strict orders not to go more than a hundred yards from our vehicles, but fortunately for us within this restricted area was a village pub and this is where we spent most evenings. There is no doubt that our arrival in the area caused a dramatic increase in the pub's beer sales.

On the evening of the 21st May, 1940 I was in that village pub with many other Queen Vics and we had been drinking solidly for about four hours when suddenly the air raid sirens started wailing. 'The Landlord won't have to kick us out tonight' said a voice from the crowd as everybody hurriedly finished their drinks and headed for the door.

In the event of an air raid warning our orders were to get to our vehicles immediately and in accordance with those orders all the soldiers were making their way along the road as quickly as they could. Admittedly many of them required a lot of help from the more sober ones, but in spite of the somewhat erratic progress a feeling of urgency seemed to be inspiring them to get back to their vehicles quickly.

Within a very short space of time the air was filled with the sound of engines as all the motorcycles, scout cars and trucks were brought to a state of readiness in case there was a paratroop drop in the area and we had to go searching for them as we had spent months in training to do. I sat in the Humber Snipe wireless truck with my colleague Roger Murray and speculated on whether we would shortly be careering around the Kent countryside or whether it would turn out to be another false alarm – and of course – moaned about the waste of good drinking time.

After about fifteen minutes we heard shouts of 'Stop all engines!' and Roger was just saying, 'another ruddy waste of time' when a head belonging to Sergeant Jack Wilson poked through the window and said 'come on look lively you two! All Company Headquarters personnel have got to load blankets and ammunition on to trucks. 'What's going on Sarg?' I asked and was told 'How the hell do I know. I only give the orders, I don't have to understand them.'

So together with all the other wireless operators, drivers, clerks and orderlies who made up the 'C' Company Headquarters personnel I began loading 30 cwt. trucks with blankets, ammunition and various other items of stores. After a couple of hours I found myself sitting on top of the stores on a truck and we were speeding along a road in convoy wondering what on earth was happening and where we were going to.

Before long the first part of the mystery was solved when the truck pulled in and stopped in the yard in front of Ashford railway station. We were told to unload the stores and carry them on to the platform where we had to load them into baggage trucks of a train standing in the station.

This took us until daybreak and Roger and I with the others had just sat down and lit cigarettes and started to enjoy a cup of tea when right on cue, as if it was a military tattoo, the remainder of the Battalion arrived.

All the wireless trucks, scout cars, Bedford 30 cwt. trucks and the motorcycles were parked in neat rows in the station yard. After a great flurry of movement and seemingly endless shouting of orders, all the Battalion embarked on the train and I found myself in a carriage with other members of 'C' Company.

There was still a great deal of speculation about our final destination but I don't think anyone believed Smudger Smith when he said, 'The Government has said that as it is wartime we've got to economise on petrol so we are going to have to leave all our vehicles in the railway station yard and go on manoeuvres by train.'

It wasn't a very long train journey and when we disembarked we discovered we were at Folkestone and we were ordered to go along the adjacent quayside and up the gangway on to a Channel steamer called the 'Maid of Kent'.

After some delay while the stores were being transferred from the train to the steamer we eventually sailed out into the English Channel and in mid-channel we rendezvoused with other Channel steamers which I later discovered had sailed from Southampton and were carrying the 2nd Battalion KRRC, and a Rifle Brigade battalion and also a squadron of tanks were aboard. These three units together with our Battalion made up the 30th Armoured Brigade.

It was at about this time that we were told that we were on a special mission and our task was to secure and hold the defences around Calais for thirty-six hours, after which we would return to England to resume our duties as a motor-cycle battalion on anti-paratroop patrol.

After the rendezvous the steamers continued towards the French coast and in a short while they were docking in Calais harbour. As soon as the gangways were in position we were disembarking and forming up in lines in front of a customs shed. The brilliant sunshine was showing up the dust and grime on the cranes and sheds in what I assume was a typical dockside scene, and I felt depressed.

Chapter 3

Baptism of Fire

Most of the Headquarters Personnel was not required to stay with HQ in our new role of rifle battalion so the platoon I was attached to was detailed to go quickly to an indicated map reference on the outskirts of Calais and set up a roadblock. After about a twenty minute march we reached our designated position and began building a roadblock with some old oil drums and timber that we found in a nearby yard. It wasn't a fortress by any stretch of the imagination but it did provide some obstruction. We had to build the block in two sections so that there was a way through for the constantly increasing stream of refugees pushing carts and old perambulators laden with as many of their worldly possessions that they could cram on to them. In many instances a bicycle was tied on top of their possessions and occasionally there were animals tied to the handles – not only dogs but cows and goats.

There were also many French soldiers on horse-drawn carts or walking. A large number of them were wounded while most of them had vacant expressions on their faces and blank looks in their eyes. They were staring straight in front of them apparently blindly following the back of the one in front with no acknowledgement of us or the road-block, and the whole procession gave the terrible and overwhelming impression of total defeat and despair.

Although the sights I saw on this first day in France were shocking and totally unexpected, they did not affect my morale mainly because I was such a naive young soldier that I did not fully appreciate the significance of what I was seeing.

I did not realise exactly what sort of army was following the refugees and soldiers along the road, and I suppose this was also due to some extent to the fact that I was not in a position to communicate with them because I did not speak French and of course there had been no access to any radio or newspapers since we left Kent.

Early the next morning we were ordered to leave the roadblock and take up a position on top of a high canal bank with orders to fire at anything that moved in the fields on the other side of the canal. From positions behind and below us French Artillery with heavy guns started firing shells over our heads with monotonous regularity.

After occupying this position for a couple of hours we saw movement in the fields opposite so we opened fire with rifles and Bren guns and almost immediately we came under heavy mortar and artillery fire. Suddenly Johnny Joyce who was lying next to me gave a shriek of pain and I said 'Are you okay?' He replied, 'My back is burning terribly' and when I looked I discovered a piece of shrapnel had cut through his battledress blouse and webbing like a knife but incredibly had hardly touched his skin. All that could be seen were some deep scratches across his back.

I told him, 'You need some repairs to your blouse and webbing but you are really lucky, look at this' and I showed him the large piece of shrapnel that had finished up be-tween us in the grass. Some of the others had not been so fortunate as us though and they were being attended to by others with field-dressings and bandages but fortunately none of them seemed to be seriously hurt.

This episode had really shaken us and made us realise that we really were involved in a war and no longer on manoeuvres.

Then a voice said, 'Look behind you' and when we turned round and looked down on to the street below us we were absolutely amazed to see a very large number of French soldiers most of whom were carrying suitcases, strolling along as if they were going on their summer holidays. It was obvious that they had no intention of taking part in any fighting and I suspect they were going home. There must have been about three hundred of them and none of them carried any weapons nor did they appear to have taken part in any fighting or even been within sight of the enemy.

The artillery fire continued in both directions but fortunately for us the Germans appeared to be trying to hit the French artillery because their shells were going well over our heads now. No targets presented themselves to us within range of our rifles so we just waited and kept a sharp lookout for any movement in the fields opposite.

In the street below some of the French soldiers had stopped and were seated on their suitcases having a rest and smoking while a heated discussion appeared to be taking place.

Nobby Clark said 'Blimey, they are having an argument over where to go for their holidays! Bloody fools like us had no option but to come to France and they're just going off and leaving us to welcome the Germans.'

Smudger Smith said 'Why don't we give them a few passing shots to remember us by?' and although most of us felt as bitter as he did we didn't take up his suggestion.

We felt even more bitter towards the French when we heard that the dockers in Calais had, despite long arguments that had continued ever since we had landed the day before, refused to unload the tanks and the steamer had sailed back to England with the tanks still on board.

The swearing and muttering about the French continued for some time but gradually it died down and the rest of the day continued with the artillery fire going in both directions and with us opening fire every time we thought we saw movement in the fields opposite. The lieutenant in charge of us detailed Smudger Smith and myself to go and see if we could scrounge some food and he gave us a rough idea of where he thought the Battalion Headquarters might be where they may have some rations for us.

We started off down the road in the direction of Calais and before long we saw a 30 cwt. Bedford truck outside a building without anybody in sight. We didn't waste any time looking for owner and Smudger, an expert mechanic, managed to get it started and so we drove off towards Calais.

We stopped and looked in several buildings without finding any food or Headquarters personnel but we never left the truck unattended in case some unscrupulous person made off with it. Eventually we came to a large shed and when we looked inside we were amazed to find a Warrant Officer looking decidedly the worse for wear. As we spoke to him he gradually keeled over on to the floor and finished up slumped with his head and shoulders resting against the wall.

This gave us the opportunity to make a thorough search of the shed which revealed several bottles of spirits – full I hasten to add unlike the empties lying near the chair that the warrant officer had been sitting on.

Our search also revealed a large box of hard tack biscuits and a few packets of cigarettes. Before starting our journey back to the canal we had a few hard tack biscuits washed down with a liberal helping of brandy and several cigarettes, we also each hid a bottle of brandy and some cigarettes in our battledress blouses and then started back feeling a lot happier than when we started the journey. When we arrived back and told the lieutenant of our success he seemed quite pleased and then he proceeded to share the proceeds out amongst the platoon and of course we accepted our share. Later that evening Smudger and I with a few friends had a good smoke and finished off the bottles of brandy which certainly helped us to while away the long night.

Early the next morning we moved to new positions covering a railway line and a main access road. Some railway wagons had been placed as obstructions across the railway lines and a few of us lay under the wagons and kept watch through the wheels while alongside the railway the Royal Artillery had set up a few field guns to act as anti-tank guns.

The news quickly spread through our position that there had been a change of plan and Winston Churchill had personally sent an order that stated we were to remain and hold Calais for as long as we possibly could, regardless of cost, because apparently our action was tying up so many German Panzer Tanks and troops that the longer we could succeed in holding Calais the better the chances were for the evacuation of troops from Dunkirk. This order rather shattered us at first but we rather naively thought that after we had held the Germans up for a few more days then it would be our turn to be evacuated back to England.

In our position we came under some deadly sniper fire which created havoc amongst us until we managed to trace it to the top of a water tower overlooking our position, and while several of us gave covering fire a couple of the chaps succeeded in getting safely across the ground and then up to the top of the tower where they took care of the sniper who was obviously a member of the so-called 'fifth column'.

We began to come under heavy artillery and mortar fire which continued throughout Friday night and there were some casualties amongst us who were taken to the rear of our positions and treated by medical orderlies, I think they were mostly shrapnel wounds.

The next morning saw an increase in the shelling and it was joined by heavy machine-gun fire which resulted in many bullets coming under the railway trucks and sounding like a massive swarm of bees as they ricocheted off the wheels and undercarriage. I have never moved so fast in my life as when I dived out from under the railway carriage – and most of the others were just as quick. Once outside we dived into a slip trench that we had dug previously for any emergencies and the present situation certainly came under that category.

Unfortunately some of the lads were not as quick as us and they sustained flesh wounds but happily none very serious. We then settled down to a system of firing with our rifles and Bren guns at the slightest movement we saw in front of us. Occasionally our fire was accompanied by the guns of the Royal Artillery and this continued for several hours.

During the afternoon I had a pleasant surprise when I was joined by Roger Murray who had been my co-wireless-operator in the Humber Snipe wireless truck when we were in Kent. Those days seemed like years ago now.

Apparently Roger had been sent to a different road block but now together with others had been brought back to join us on this apparently strategic and important position. We had quite a reunion and Roger, Smudger and I celebrated with the last drop of brandy and some cigarettes during a relatively quiet spell. The shelling and spasmodic small arms fire continued throughout Saturday night and towards dawn Roger and Smudger disappeared to answer the call of nature amongst the bushes. Shortly after they had left the position the shelling and mortar fire intensified and some were landing too close for comfort.

It was now getting lighter and Smudger reappeared but there was no sign of Roger. Smudger said they had separated over by some bushes and he had not seen him since. I needed to go now so I went in the direction of the bushes that Smudger had pointed out which was about thirty yards away but I saw no sign of Roger although I did see many shell craters and much debris that I had not seen before.

We were told that a destroyer had come into Calais harbour during the night, and had landed reinforcements and had taken on board the wounded. This news cheered us up a bit and we were hoping that as well as a big increase in manpower, they had also brought several anti-tank guns and heavy machine guns and mortars.

Shortly after we heard this news we were told to pack up and make our way to the main railway station so after making another quick unsuccessful search for Roger we started out.

While we were on our way we heard that the reinforcements totalled seventy Royal Marines and they had only brought enough guns for themselves and these did not include any heavy guns.

Although we had the greatest admiration for the fighting qualities of the Royal Marines, we thought their contribution would be as useful as trying to empty the English Channel with a teaspoon.

When we arrived at the railway station we were directed into the buffet rooms and each collected a mug of tea and some hard tack biscuits. We unloaded our equipment and sat down to relax and tried really hard to imagine we had a large plateful of fish and chips instead of a measly handful of hard tack biscuits but even our imagination couldn't stretch that far.

I had just finished drinking my tea when there was a terrible shrieking noise and bombs started falling on the railway station. The huge glass windows all round the buffet rooms shattered and there were pieces of glass flying all over the place. Instinctively I had dived under the table and I lay there listening as all hell broke loose with the noise of falling bombs exploding and the terrifying wailing of the Stuka bombers diving on to their target. I thought I was the marker in the middle of the target area and that every pilot was carrying out a personal vendetta against me.

A sergeant major began shouting, 'Everybody on their feet and get outside' so rather bewildered we staggered outside on to a platform and following the sergeant major's orders we lined up on the edge of the platform and commenced firing at the Stukas diving down at us.

I will always remember seeing the sergeant major shouting filthy obscenities at the planes and at the same time holding a Bren gun to his shoulder and firing at them. He never stopped swearing or firing for at least twenty minutes and although this small-arms fire may not have brought any planes down, it did at least help us to overcome the shock of the sudden attack and it went some way to restoring our confidence. We left the shambles of the railway station behind us with medical orderlies attending to the wounded whilst we went in small groups to take up positions in the town. I was threading my way through debris and damaged vehicles in the railway yard when for some unaccountable reason I had this strong, irresistible feeling that I must stop behind a derelict tank to light a cigarette. While I was getting my cigarettes out and preparing to light one two other chaps went past me.

I was just lighting the cigarette when there was a terrific bang as a shell or bomb landed in the yard. The blast knocked me off my feet and as I lay there stunned for several minutes it was obvious that the tank had protected me and saved me from serious injury. Despite being a member of the Church Lads Brigade when I was younger I was not particularly religious, but I thought then that some person or power must have made me stop for that cigarette and had possibly saved my life.

I managed to stagger to my feet but it was still very difficult to see very much because of the clouds of dust still swirling around. As it gradually cleared I could see a large crater and debris everywhere yet I couldn't find any trace of the two men who had gone past me.

This narrow escape really shook me but I managed to pull myself together and then joined some other chaps. We went into a large house and took up positions at some upstairs windows overlooking a square. Within a few minutes we saw German soldiers appear round a corner and we started firing at them but this only resulted in us coming under fire from tanks and then continuous mortar fire which forced us to leave that position and draw back through other houses.

We were stopping in other positions and firing at the Germans but after several hours of this fighting against overwhelming odds we withdrew, taking the wounded with us but leaving several dead behind. We then took up a position in an old coastal gun emplacement overlooking the town. Below us was a canal and on the other side of the canal was a field in the middle of which was the Old Citadel which had been taken over by our Battalion Headquarters.

From this latest position we had a good view of the streets below and whenever any German soldiers showed themselves we opened fire. There was no point in wasting ammunition on Panzers and although we must have inflicted many casualties amongst the foot soldiers it did not seem to be having any effect on the speed of the German advance.

There was a major from the Rifle Brigade who, although wounded in the leg and the arm, was standing on top of the gun emplacement shouting and encouraging us to keep on fighting. He was without doubt the bravest man I have ever seen. But despite his encouragement and bravery there came a time when the situation became hopeless.

The predicament we were in resulted from the fact that the Germans had advanced along the other side of the canal and gained control of the Citadel. This enabled them to fire into our unprotected backs and although we continued firing until our ammunition ran out, there was no way of escape from our position. We had to bow to the inevitable and surrender.

Before we surrendered we threw our rifle bolts into the canal and smashed our rifles against the gun emplacement concrete surround to make sure that they could not be used by the enemy. The major then signalled to the Germans that we were surrendering and they motioned for us to come down and cross a small bridge over the canal to the field by the Citadel. There we joined a group of our comrades lying on the grass. As I lay there thoroughly exhausted, dejected and so miserable I cannot find the right words to express it, I saw one of our officers with tears in his eyes looking absolutely shattered. He appeared to be looking at us without seeing us and his expression was one of total disbelief and utter sadness.

It was the afternoon of Sunday 26th May, 1940 and although we had accomplished our original task of holding Calais for thirty-six hours (in fact we had held it for four days against overwhelming odds) nevertheless we still felt let down. We were convinced that if we had come over with our own transport and with a reasonable amount of supporting fire power, food and equipment, and most importantly a continuous supply of ammunition, we could have achieved much more.

I am finding it very difficult to put into words how I felt during the period immediately following my capture. I was filled with despair, utterly dejected and thoroughly drained of any strength, but at the same time there was a strong feeling of anger at the way we had been used and let down and, to be quite honest, sacrificed.

We certainly at no time felt inferior to the Germans and were convinced that a fair chance with arms and equipment of the same standard or similar, we were more than a match for them.

After a time the Germans told us to throw our tin helmets, webbing and any arms into a big heap and then they searched us, confiscating watches and other personal possessions. They seemed to take great pleasure in constantly repeating to us, 'For you the war is over' which certainly annoyed us and did nothing at all to lift our spirits or make us feel better.

Shortly after this degrading procedure we were ordered to start marching and we went through the town of Calais, passing many scenes of destruction and seeing several positions that we had attempted to hold.

Most of the buildings we had been in were totally destroyed and there were heaps of rubble in the road and across the pavements which we had to go round or climb over them. There were a couple of lorries taking our wounded and eventually we reached a churchyard where we were told we were going to spend the night. All those who had been walking prepared to settle down but the lorries continued their journey, presumably to a hospital.

Chapter 4

First Days as POW

Before we could even lie down a German officer told us in very good English that volunteers were needed to return to Calais because there were several of our comrades lying wounded and they needed to be found and transported to hospital. About thirty of us clambered on to the back of a truck and were taken back to Calais. By the time we arrived it was getting dark and we were shepherded into a block of flats for the night. I was lucky enough to find a king-size bed with a lovely feather mattress and I collapsed exhausted on to it and fell asleep almost immediately. It was the best sleep I had had for ages and certainly since I had gone to Ashford railway station to load the train.

Early the next morning we were rudely awakened by shouts of 'Raus' and when it dawned on us where we were and that we were prisoners of war, we became filled with despair and were thoroughly depressed. Going downstairs I felt mentally drained even though I had had such a long sleep. When we reached the ground floor we were given a bowl of watery soup by the Germans and told to line up in the courtyard outside. There was a lot of shouting which none of us could understand and then some German officers arrived. One of them looked like a typical Prussian Officer from the cinema (he even had a monocle in his right eye). One of the officers started walking down the line of prisoners, stopping and showing a postcard to each of the prisoners while the Prussian type, who appeared to be the senior officer there, kept a close watch on our facial expressions.

A whisper 'Don't laugh' went down the ranks preceding the officer showing the postcard and when he showed it to me I realised the reason for the warning. The picture was a cartoon of a Tommy sticking his bayonet up the rear end of Adolf Hitler. With much difficulty, we succeeded in controlling ourselves and saved ourselves from punishment by the Germans. Shortly afterwards we were taken in small groups under armed guard, mistakenly thinking we were going to search for wounded. But we were soon disillusioned and the truth of that old Army saying 'Never Volunteer' was brought home to us once more.

The truth was that there were no wounded still waiting for attention and instead we had to bury some of our comrades who had been killed in action. We also had to bury dead horses and clear some of the heaps of rubble. The next morning started with the same procedure but a couple of us managed to avoid the guards and behind some sand dunes we found a small wireless truck which had been abandoned, and after climbing' inside we attempted to get the radio to work so that we could try and make contact with someone in England. All our efforts were in vain because we had just exhausted our attempts to get it working when there were loud shouts from some German guards who threatened us with their guns and left us in no doubt that they wanted us out of the truck immediately. They took us back to where the remainder of the prisoners were working, prodding and hitting us with their rifles.

We had to continue with the clearing up and from that moment on there always seemed to be a guard paying particular attention to us two but the evening arrived at last and we returned to the flats and the bowl of watery soup after which there was nothing to do but to settle down to sleep.

The next morning we were clearing up outside a building when we realised that the ground floor had been a seedy-looking bar I managed to slip inside without attracting any guard's attention and found several bottles of red wine which I stuffed inside my battledress blouse and told the others so that they could each take it in turns to go inside and get some bottles too.

That evening on our return to the flats we thought we might as well get drunk to forget our problems for a while. I took just one sip and had to spit it out because it tasted like vinegar. Nevertheless, some of the chaps persevered with it and succeeded in getting very drunk.

We were told that we would be leaving Calais and without any further warning were marching through the town of Calais once again and after walking for several miles joined up with a long column of British and French prisoners which was following two trucks containing several wounded prisoners.

At that time I did not realise that this was to be the start of a long and tedious march that would take us in circles round Northern France, along the border of Luxembourg and into Belgium. The prisoners were being continually pushed and harassed by the guards to keep them moving as quickly as possible and we were averaging about forty kilometres a day. French civilians often put buckets of water out for us but the guards always kicked them over to stop us from getting a drink and since no food was being provided we were getting very hungry and thirsty.

We had not had a good meal since leaving England and it got to the stage when we were so desperate that we began to take chances to get anything to eat. One day there were about thirty of us chasing chickens round a farmyard with the German guards in hot pursuit, firing their guns in the air. Eventually they managed to get us into some semblance of order and we were again marching along the road. A trail of chicken feathers along the road was sufficient proof that some prisoners had been successful and fortunately for me Nobby Clark, one of our gang, had been one of the fitter prisoners who had been fast enough to catch a chicken. Since I had been lucky enough to find some eggs in a chicken house we had a really good meal that night which we ate like the pack of hungry savages that we had become.

On another occasion I sustained a three-inch gash on my wrist through climbing over a barbed wire fence to pick some gooseberries. We also frequently dived into fields to quickly dig up some potatoes, which, because we were so hungry, we often chewed raw while walking along the road.

Whilst marching along one day I could not help noticing a Frenchman who was clinging on to a small suitcase as if it contained the Crown Jewels and it looked as if it was strapped to his wrist with a leather belt. I pointed this out to Nobby and said, 'He must have something really valuable in there, maybe it's a ham sandwich'.

Nobby replied 'It might be worth our while to keep an eye on him and if we get a chance we'll have a look inside'.

For the rest of that day we watched the Frenchman like hawks and when we eventually marched into a field for the night stop we made sure that we laid down a short distance from him so that we could watch him. A few hours later when the only sounds and movements were the German guards patrolling round the perimeter of the field which was illuminated by lamps and occasionally by the headlights of the trucks. Nobby turned to me and said, 'Its time we made a move' and three of us started to crawl across the grass towards our mystery case-carrier and after several stoppages because of sounds and movements from figures lying on the ground, we eventually reached our objective.

The third member of our gang, Jack Wiltshire, stopped a few yards away ready to create a diversion if necessary and Nobby and I crawled close to the Frenchman. I was prepared to hit him with a rock I had picked up on the way if he gave the slightest sign of waking up whilst Nobby carefully cut through the leather belt attached to the Frenchman's wrist and we then slowly and carefully crawled away with the suitcase. When we had reached what we considered to be a safe distance from the Frenchman we opened the case and found that we had hit the jackpot because among a lot of papers which it was too dark to read (and they couldn't be eaten anyway) we found several bars of Cadbury's chocolate and four packets of Players cigarettes.

After sharing out the proceeds of our little expedition we crawled away leaving the suitcase by the side of a sleeping figure, and in the morning while we were breakfasting on the chocolate and enjoying a cigarette, Nobby said, 'We have nothing to be ashamed of; they were NAAFI issue and we are more entitled to them than some stinking Froggie.'

Just as Nobby finished talking there was a terrible commotion because the Frenchman had just woken up and realised he no longer had the case attached to his wrist. A few minutes later there was an even bigger row when he discovered the missing case by the side of a Moroccan and because of our disillusionment with the majority of the French troops we wouldn't have shed any tears if they had injured each other. After a lot of arm waving and shouting the Frenchman took his case back to where he had been lying and we watched him still talking loudly and gesticulating to a Frenchman near him. Perhaps it was a good thing we didn't understand much French because I'm sure that some of his language was too rude for nice clean-living Englishmen to hear.

The seemingly endless march continued day after day and we got the distinct impression that we were going round in circles. Invariably when we tried to ask the guards how much further each day they always signalled that the end was just round the next corner.

During another night's stop (this time it was in a civilian prison, I think a place called Fresnes) there was almost a riot when some Moroccans tried to sell Cadbury's chocolate and English cigarettes to anyone with sufficient francs to pay their exorbitant prices.

Since we had never received any francs we were not in the market anyway, but in any case their having the cheek to try and sell to us what we regarded as our rightful property caused several of us to lose our tempers and fighting soon broke out all over the prison. Anything that could inflict injury was used as a weapon including iron bars, pieces of wood, belts and knives. Before long there were bodies lying all over the place.

I was lucky in that I had no serious injuries or broken bones – only a few bruises – but unfortunately I didn't succeed in getting my hands on any chocolate or cigarettes either and neither did my pals. The next morning there were several signs of the fighting but as far as I know everybody was able to continue on the march although we were very pleased to see that the French and the Moroccans appeared to have suffered far more than any of us.

Eventually we arrived at Bastogne in Belgium and for the very first time the Germans offered us some food, which turned out to be a small piece of pork fat and a small slice of black mouldy bread. Although I was very hungry I could not eat the pork fat and after several unsuccessful attempts I gave it to Nobby Clark who gobbled it up as if it was best fillet steak.

We were marched to the railway station and there we saw a stationary train consisting of a long line of cattle trucks and a couple of passenger carriages. The guards shouted and pushed us towards the trucks and I counted seventy of us in our truck before the door was slammed shut. The only ventilation was through a small opening high on the side of the truck and this was covered by barbed wire.

It was a slow, seemingly endless journey interspersed by shuntings but no actual stops. The lack of fresh air and the stench of urine and so many unwashed bodies all crammed together in such a small space made it almost unbearable, and I personally would far rather have been on the road marching. Finally the train came to a halt and after some delay the doors were opened and the guards motioned us to get out on to the platform. The signs on the platform told us it was a place called Trier and some knowledgeable fellow told us it was a town on the German border and it was on the banks of the Rhine. Leaving the railway yards we were marched through the town (fortunately I was in the middle of the column) when suddenly we were being showered with stones thrown at us by the German civilians, mostly women, who were lining the pavements. Some unfortunate prisoners closest to the pavement took the full brunt of the missile attack and the spittle aimed at them by the violent women.

That night we slept in some old cavalry barracks, and much to our surprise we were given a bowl of watery soup and a small portion of mouldy black bread. Next morning after a quick wash under a cold water tap we were ushered out of the barracks and through the town where, once again, we had to run the gauntlet of the missile throwing civilians as we went back to the railway yards and the awful cattle trucks. After a short delay we were all on board and the journey continued in the same terrible cramped, crowded conditions as before.

Due to the lack of toilet facilities, poor ventilation and overcrowding, the truck became Hell on Earth. For me the oppressive stench was sickening and any semblance of human dignity became a thing of the past.

Chapter 5
Prison Camp in Poland

The journey finally came to an end when we arrived at a place called Thorn in Poland. The cattle trucks disgorged their cargo of miserable, filthy and wretched prisoners on to the platform, many of whom were too weak to stand because of illness, the lack of food, inhuman conditions and near suffocation endured on the long journey, and several collapsed on to the ground.

It was not the first time that many of us thought that we might be better off dead, nor would it be the last, but overriding all this was the human instinct for survival and we all managed to stagger to our feet and start walking along the road with many being supported by those who were stronger.

The final destination turned out to be an old Polish fort and in the grounds surrounding the actual fort were rows of large marquees to which we were directed. Once inside we found rows of straw palliasses on the ground and we thankfully fell down on to the nearest unoccupied one.

Before long the German guards were coming through the marquees prodding with their rifles and shouting at us to get up and go outside where we were shepherded on to a large parade ground and then lined up. While the Germans were walking up and down counting us, I looked round at the tall, double wire fence with watch towers at intervals that surrounded the whole complex of the fort and the marquees. When they finished counting and had finally agreed on a figure we were marched in to the main fort building.

When we got inside we were pushed one by one into a small room to have our photographs taken. I hadn't shaved since leaving England and by now had an untidy beard and being unwashed too looked thoroughly disreputable.

When my turn came to go into the room a numbered board was held in front of me whilst the photograph was taken, and then I was issued with a metal disc on which the same number as that on the board was repeated on the top and bottom half. I was told it must be worn round the neck at all times.

I was now officially prisoner of war number 10706 and I wore this disc together with my British Army dog tags on a piece of cord round my neck.

Nobby Clark said, 'As we always travel in cattle trucks I suppose we ought to be thankful that they haven't stapled the disc through our nose or ears'. We soon got into a daily routine which consisted of lining up on the parade ground for early morning roll-call which invariably turned out to be a long-drawn-out affair because the Germans always appeared to have difficulty in counting large numbers of men and matching the figures with the lists they carried.

This delay annoyed us intensely because it meant we were unable to go and queue for our breakfast which was always a mug of ersatz coffee (barely drinkable). All the hardened smokers used to save the coffee (?) grounds and when they were dry used them as a substitute for tobacco.

After breakfast the mornings were spent lying on our palliasses and at midday we queued for a bowl of watery soup. If you were very fortunate you found a small piece of potato in it and if you were very quick and very lucky you could queue again and get a second helping.

This meagre meal seemed to give us just enough energy to get back to our palliasses for another sleep until the late afternoon when it would be time for another roll call. After another irritating session of innumerable counts by the Germans we would scramble into another queue to get our main meal of the day which consisted of a loaf of black bread to be shared among six men.

Since there was no honour among starving men, you clung to your group of six and in particular made certain that the chap carrying the bread never got out of your sight because if you were even foolish enough to blink, you ran the risk of losing your bread ration. The actual sharing of the bread always involved a long discussion on the best and fairest way of cutting the bread so that everyone got an absolutely equal share but in the end it usually came down to a draw to determine the order of choice.

Although many prisoners tried all sorts of desperate tricks to try and steal bread from the truck I cannot recall a single successful attempt mainly because there was always a ring of guards with dogs surrounding the truck. I tried once or twice but I can tell you from bitter experience that those dogs were very quick and decidedly unfriendly.

One morning we staggered out for roll-call as usual and in accordance with the normal practice the British were along one side with the Polish lined up at right angles to them and opposite the British with about fifty yards between them were the French. The camp Commandant with his entourage marched on to the parade ground and announced through his three interpreters that France had capitulated. Immediately the French, wrongly assuming they would soon be on their way home very quickly started cheering and dancing.

This show of pleasure by the French at the fall of their country so incensed the British that they broke ranks and ran across the parade ground and we were soon throwing punches, although in all honesty we were so weak that we couldn't have broken the skin on a rice pudding. While this fracas was going on the Poles stared in disbelief at the scene and the Commandant was screaming something in German we couldn't understand, in any case none of us were in a mood to listen to him. But when the guards started firing machine guns just over our heads we quickly understood the message and the fighting stopped.

The guards, with their bayonets and rifle butts managed to get us back in some semblance of order. The Commandant was still shouting and waving his arms about but eventually he calmed down and through the interpreters told us that if there was any recurrence of this disgraceful behaviour we would either be shot or sent to a Strafelager (punishment camp).

A couple of days passed before anything further unusual happened and this was when we were taken into the main fort buildings again. We were lined up along a corridor and told to strip to the waist, and when we arrived at the head of the queue an orderly stuck an hypodermic needle into our chest. I maintain that the one that was stuck in me had been used hundreds of times before because it felt like an old sword. Anyway, for whatever reason, I immediately passed out and fell to the floor. I came round with a couple of the chaps holding my head under an old-fashioned water pump which certainly succeeded in bringing me round. However, for at least a week afterwards my chest was very sore and severely bruised.

Fainting was not an unusual occurrence now and men often passed out because of the lack of a proper diet. Frequently someone would get up to go somewhere and then just without any warning, collapse unconscious, and we would put him on his palliasse to recover.

Eventually this became such a frequent occurrence that we just used to ignore them and leave them to recover of their own accord which they usually did within a few minutes. They would then struggle to get up and stagger off to wherever they wanted to go to although it had been known on a few occasions for them to forget where they had been headed for and they just returned to their palliasse.

There were occasions when a prisoner would collapse outside the marquee and someone would look at them to make sure it was just a faint. If they seemed okay they were left to recover by themselves.

I was in the marquee with a chap who maintained he was a lord and a real member of the aristocracy. Whether this was true or not I never did bother to find out, but some believed him. He made a habit of getting the men to run errands for him such as fetching his coffee and soup and he even managed on occasion to get them to give him their bread ration. For payment he rewarded them with IOUs written on scraps of paper. Before I left the camp I knew of one chap who held IOUs to the value of £10,000, but whether he ever managed to keep all the pieces of paper and then managed to redeem them after the war I do not know. To heavy smokers like myself, the shortage of tobacco was at least as big a problem as the food shortage. Outside our marquee there grew a small tree which I jealously guarded.

I used to pick the leaves and dry them in the sun, and then after a few hours I used to roll them in my hands and use the leaves as a tobacco mixture. It tasted absolutely ghastly but it did serve to satisfy my craving.

Except perhaps for heavy smokers like myself, all other cravings faded into insignificance when compared to a desperate longing for food. This was illustrated by the fact that although normally when a group of men got together, particularly soldiers, the main topics of conversation are sex, dirty jokes or sometimes beer.

In the prison camp at Thorn the only real topic of conversation was food and the usual subjects were never mentioned. Groups of prisoners often sat around discussing possible ways of breaking into the German stores or stealing a loaf of bread from the delivery cart, but despite a multitude of ideas, some clever and some really weird, as far as I know there were no successful thefts.

The Germans required us to write our names and peace time occupations on a list but what they thought of the completed lists I never found out but I imagine they were surprised to find they had captured some strange prisoners. The lists showed Tom Mix – Cowboy, Mickey Mouse – cheese collector, Dr Jekyll – quick change artist, Tiny Tim – flea circus trainer, and also there were the following occupations: airline pilot, food taster, brothel keeper, Big Ben winder, cooks and chefs.

Apparently no action was taken over the lists and I don't think anyone managed to get a job or even an interview for the jobs they had listed. There were a lot of rumours going round the camp about everybody being sent out on working parties and we were all wondering where we would be going.

Chapter 6

Pub With No Beer

The general opinion seemed to be that if you were a farmer or even a farm labourer you would get plenty of food if you were sent to work on a farm so of course when the next list appeared everybody had been a farmer or farm labourer or in one or two instances, a shepherd or cowman.

The time finally arrived when they started to send prisoners away to other camps to go out on working parties but this did not seem to have been based on the lists. My turn came to depart from camp and together with about two hundred others I marched to the railway station. To our amazement there were no first-class carriages and instead we had to climb up into the inevitable cattle trucks. At the end of another uncomfortable journey we found ourselves at Danzig railway station.

We left the station and marched along a wide road which from a sign fixed to the side of a building we knew was called Friedrichstrasse. After walking for about a mile we were stopped outside a dilapidated building. Over the main door was a large sign with the paint peeling from it but we could see that it used to be a Beer Garden.

Our first reaction was that it was marvellous to be billeted in a Beer Garden but as we went through the main door into what had obviously been the bar we were quickly disillusioned. The actual bar was behind a strong wire fence which was suspended from strong timber struts fixed from

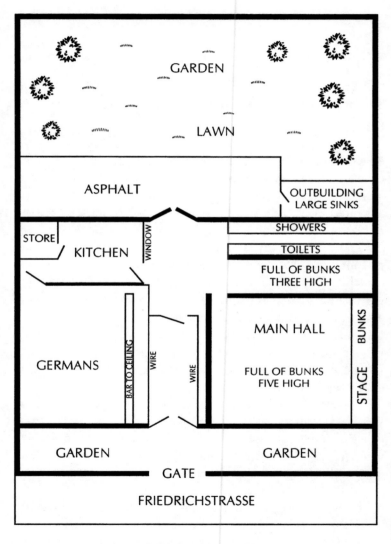

Plan of the Old Beer Garden

floor to ceiling. There were no bottles to be seen behind the bar and certainly nobody offered us a drink.

About five feet from the bar was another wire fence constructed in the same manner and going through a gate in this fence we came to an opening on the right which led into a very large hall at the end of which there was a stage. However, the entire floor space, including the stage, was filled with wooden bunks five high with gangways between of only about one foot and the main access gangway being approximately two feet wide.

On the right-hand walls very high up were some small windows which were securely fastened and covered on the outside with a strong metal mesh. These windows looked out on Friedrichstrasse and apart from the doorway entrance were the only means of ventilation for the whole hall.

Another opening next to the entrance to the hall led to a long, narrow room which was also filled with wooden bunks three high separated by narrow gangways, I quickly claimed one of the top bunks because I figured that the inconvenience of continually climbing up to the top bunk was infinitely better than being frequently showered with dust and dirt from the bunks above you or being trodden on by the occupants of the top bunks. Another door from the front area led into a long room containing wash basins and toilets. Since there were no partitions, any vestiges of dignity left after the march and our stay at Thorn were quickly dispelled. Next to this room was yet another doorway leading to a back garden but this entrance was always kept securely locked and barred except when we were paraded for roll calls or occasionally allowed to use it for an exercise area.

These exercise periods were usually on a Sunday because on all other days we would be out on our working parties, and whenever prisoners were out in the back garden for roll-call or exercise it was always patrolled by armed guards.

The remainder of the building, which was separated from the prisoners' quarters, was also surrounded by a strong wire fence and consisted of a kitchen, food store and accommodation for the Commandant and the guards.

All the above information was explained to us before we were given a fifth of a loaf of black bread each. There was no question of choosing or dividing the loaves ourselves, we had to take whatever we were given. If you were lucky you got a good-sized piece otherwise; hard luck. With this bread we received a bowl of soup which actually had some small pieces of potato in it.

This was a big improvement on our previous rations and we foolishly thought that this was paradise and that our luck had changed at last. At 5.45 the next morning came the rude awakening when the German guards walked up and down the main gangways, banging on the beds and shouting for us all to get up immediately and get out into the back garden for roll-call. The guards were even pulling some of the prisoners out of their bunks, others were pushing us to the back door and when we reached the garden they pushed us into lines. As usual it took the Germans about five counts before they were satisfied that none of us had disappeared during the night.

This was the first real opportunity to look round the garden since I arrived and I saw it was roughly one hundred yards square and that the part nearest to the building on which we paraded for roll-call was covered in asphalt. Surrounding this section was a large lawn which had various shrubs and trees around it and the whole garden was enclosed by a high wall with rolls of barbed wire strung along the top of it.

After this first roll-call we had to queue for the inevitable mug of ersatz coffee but we barely had time to drink any of it before we were being shouted at to line up. Then we were marched out through the former bar into Friedrichstrasse then round the side of the building on to a footpath which went through a large field and up to the top of a hill which we discovered was called Stolzenberg. Although we were unaware of it then, this was in the future destined to become our home for a long time.

Upon reaching the summit the guards lined us up and some civilians appeared and started to distribute spades, shovels and pickaxes to us. They then directed us to where there were pegs in the ground and told us to dig trenches between the pegs and from one larger peg to another; the trench was to be two feet deep. There was no question of slackening and leaning on our shovels because there were armed guards as well as civilians who certainly did not refrain from showing their hatred of us. Believe me the feeling was mutual. Although the guards were also un-friendly, I must admit they did not show any favouritism and they seemed to take great pleasure in using their bayonets and rifle butts on all of us at some time or other. I certainly collected some bruises on that first day.

Some of the prisoners were given the task of digging and constructing primitive latrines which consisted of a long pole suspended over a large pit about twelve feet long. Whenever prisoners had to answer the call of nature they were accompanied by an armed guard to ensure there was no unnecessary delay in returning to work.

Apart from a short break at midday, during which we discovered that we were supposed to have saved some of our bread ration from the previous evening to eat for our lunch, we continued working until six o'clock, and after returning the tools which were counted and locked up in a wooden shed we were marched back down the hill to the old Beer Garden.

About half an hour after our return we were issued with our bread ration and a bowl of potato soup which was gulped down by nearly everybody. As a result of the exhausting work and our poor physical condition due to the insufficient diet, we could only stagger to our bunks and collapse on to them. Within a very short space of time there was absolute silence in the building except for a few snores and grunts.

The next day started with the same routine but this time all the prisoners did their best to 'help' the Germans with their counting so that we could delay our start up the hill as long as possible, but eventually the Germans managed to get it right and off we went up the hill.

During the day everyone was trying to devise methods of avoiding work or at least doing as little as possible without attracting the unwelcome attentions of the guards and their rifles. But although the guards always had difficulty in counting, they seemed to be able to hit us without any trouble at all.

This became the daily routine but before long we had another very annoying problem. To put it bluntly, we were all lousy. From then on it became a normal sight in the evenings to see prisoners sitting on their bunks examining the linings of their shirts and trousers inch by inch and killing as many lice as they could find. Frequently during the night I would be driven to desperation by the continual itching and would then have to join other sufferers in the room with wash basins and toilets which was the only place on our side of the wire that had lights left on during the night. We would carry out extensive searches of our clothing in the hope that we could exterminate enough of the little blighters so that we could return to our bunks and get some sleep before the horrible guards came along, shouting and banging.

The next Sunday morning after roll-call and coffee we were pushed out of the front of the building into Friedrichstrasse and after being lined up in some semblance of order we started marching towards the centre of Danzig. A voice said 'The nice Germans are taking us to the railway station for a ride into the country for a picnic' and somebody replied, 'Don't be silly it's Sunday and we are going to a church service': In the event both were wrong because we were marched straight past the railway station and several churches until finally on the outskirts of Danzig we were taken into a large building which we soon discovered was a delousing station.

Once inside we were ordered to strip and all our clothes were put into huge machines with liquid inside them smelling of strong chemicals Obviously this process was intended to kill off all the lice and any other creatures and while this process was going on we were taken in front of a team of barbers.

The barbers used clippers and cut-throat razors to remove every hair from our heads and bodies and their far from gentle administrations left several of us with cuts and scrapes in some very tender places. After this very painful experience we were given small squares of sandstone, masquerading as soap, then pushed into a large room with scalding hot water pouring from overhead outlets.

Although it was extremely difficult to get any lather from the so-called soap, at least after a good scrub we felt cleaner than we had done for a long time. We left the shower room and in another room we tried to dry ourselves on our very small towels. Then after finding our clothes amongst a huge heap of clothes that had been dumped on the floor we struggled to get dressed. It was very difficult because they still felt damp and our bodies were not properly dry, and to add to our discomfort the clothes were giving off a very strong smell of the chemicals used to disinfect them.

My feelings were mixed as we set off for the camp: on the one hand I was very glad that I felt cleaner, but I was very sore from the attentions of the barber and I felt very cold because I had been unable to dry myself properly. The damp clothes felt very uncomfortable but the strangest feeling was one of nakedness caused by my shaven head.

Arriving back at the old Beer Garden we discovered that the whole camp had been thoroughly fumigated which meant we should be able to look forward to at least a few weeks without lice.

The next break from normal routine came when we were issued with clothes supposedly to enable us to withstand the oncoming harsh winter.

My issue was comprised of a Polish Army cloth cap, a Belgian Army greatcoat so old and thin that you could see daylight through it, two small squares of cloth for use as foot rags in place of socks and a pair of wooden clogs. Initially I found it very difficult to walk in the clogs but after some practice I found I could walk in them almost as well as in my old boots, but any attempt at clog dancing always ended in chaos.

An important milestone in our life in captivity occurred one evening when, after drawing our bread ration, we had to line up in the back garden and were told that some Red Cross parcels had arrived but were so few in number that only very small portions of food could be given to each prisoner. So while I stood there with my piece of bread held in front of me members of the kitchen staff came round and in turn deposited a thin slice of luncheon meat, a spoonful of jam and a tiny portion of fish on it, I must agree that it sounds a very queer mixture but it made a very welcome and appetising meal.

We were now allowed to write postcards and were told that lists of our names had been given to representatives of the International Red Cross, but it was to be a very long time before we received any letters from home. One morning during our march up the hill a nice-looking young woman passed us on the way down and when she drew level she said in a friendly voice, 'Guten morgen'. Unfortunately at that time in the morning and in our depressed state of mind we were in no mood for early morning politeness and several of the lads gave the morning greeting normally reserved for the German guards: 'Bollocks'.

Meeting the same young lady every morning meant that the same greetings became a regular occurrence and to our astonishment one morning she, obviously thinking it was the usual British greeting in the mornings, said, 'Bollocks' and after recovering and realising what she had said all the prisoners burst out laughing and there was a chorus of 'Bollocks' in return. It proved to be a real talking point and really brightened up our morning.

This method of greeting became normal practice and whenever we had new additions to our ranks everybody tried to get into a position where we could watch the faces of the newcomers when the young lady gave the usual greeting as it was very amusing to see the look of astonishment on their faces. The continual monotonous and miserable existence made up of long hours of backbreaking work, little food and living in a strange unfriendly environment and the uncertainty of not knowing what was happening to our family and friends back home created a big strain and undoubtedly began to have an effect on us mentally.

One day this pressure culminated in a Welsh Guardsman called Taffy Williams exploding and hitting a German guard with a shovel. Before any of us could react another guard had shot Taffy. There was chaos with prisoners' tempers at boiling point but the other guards had quickly surrounded the area and stood threatening the other prisoners with their guns. The ugly situation eventually calmed down a bit and we carried Taffy's body back to the camp. For a few days it was touch and go whether there would be a full scale riot.

I think the Germans realised what a delicate situation it was and kept a relatively low profile, thus avoiding another incident likely to spark off any more trouble, about four days after the shooting there was a military funeral with six prisoners acting as a guard of honour at the graveside.

In the camp afterwards there was naturally a very depressing atmosphere. Running through it all there was a feeling of anger at the Germans, but in a strange way we also felt anger at ourselves because we had not really been in a position to have done anything about it, and we had not realised how near the edge Taffy had been and so we had been unable to prevent the tragedy. Since the shooting we had not seen any of the guards involved and can only assume that the Commandant had thought it best to send them away as soon as possible. It was some time before things began to get back to some semblance of order but life had to go on. In our situation I suppose the loss of a life would not be unusual.

The Germans began taking great delight in telling us how the marvellous Luftwaffe was bombing London and other major cities to the ground and how the glorious U-boats were sinking all the British shipping in the Atlantic. After a time this continuous badgering began to have an effect on us but we kept telling each other that it was only German propaganda and we would start beating the bastards soon.

Chapter 7

First Escape – First Christmas

The first snows of winter arrived and increasingly the bitter weather combined with the meagre food rations we were given, added to the general feeling of depression and hopelessness. It must have been these feelings that made four of us make what must have been one of the most ill-conceived and stupid attempts to escape that had ever been made.

It all started on one Sunday afternoon when we were strolling in the back garden and stamping our feet and clapping our hands together to keep warm. Despite the weather we were glad to be out in the open air with an illusory feeling of freedom when Dai Jones said, 'Bugger this, I can't stand it anymore. Let's go over the wall'. Nobby Clark replied, 'Why not. If we go down to that end of the garden, the wall is slightly lower and we could use the lower branches of a tree to help us get over and the shrubs down there will give us good cover'. After a few more circuits of the garden arguing over the possibilities and giving that end of the garden a careful scrutiny and watching the position of the guards, we finally all agreed to give it a try. Looking back on it I feel that we must have had a rush of blood to the brain but at the time we were so desperate that it seemed like a good idea.

The four of us strolled casually down to that end of the garden and when some of the chaps obligingly distracted the guards, we all managed to scramble up and over the wall and the barbed wire with only a few minor scratches and a few tears in our clothes which were so shabby it hardly made any difference.

Our first objective was to get as far away from the camp as quickly as possible. Unfortunately the weather was deteriorating by the minute and it was fast approaching blizzard conditions. Nevertheless we felt that now we had taken the plunge there was no going back at least not willingly.

After scrambling and sliding across fields through the snow for what we estimated to be about five miles and we were just about coming to the end of our tether when we spotted a small wooden hut and we decided to investigate. After breaking into the hut we decided we would have to shelter there for a few hours in the hope that the weather would improve and that the rest might help us to recover our strength.

Inside we found a table, wooden benches and a small iron stove with some kindling on the floor beside it. Fortunately Nobby had some matches and we soon got a fire going which very quickly made the small hut very warm and cosy.

Because of the struggle through the snow and because we had not been getting sufficient food for some time we were all thoroughly exhausted and this, combined with the lovely warmth in the hut, made us all feel very drowsy. The urge to sleep became irresistible and within a few minutes we were all fast asleep.

Our peaceful sleep was rudely shattered by the sound of the door crashing open and by the loud snarling and barking of large German shepherd dogs. I reluctantly opened my eyes and saw two German guards inside the hut and two vicious dogs snarling and baring their teeth at us from the doorway; fortunately their handlers appeared to have control of them.

The shouting and actions of the German guards left us in no doubt that they wanted us up and out of the hut and after a few hard blows from their rifle butts we didn't argue.

When we got outside we saw several more guards and dogs so we resigned ourselves to a very uncomfortable walk back to the camp. The guards by the frequent use of their rifle butts made it abundantly clear that having to leave their own warm accommodation to go searching in a blizzard for some stupid prisoners was not their idea of a pleasant Sunday evening. We arrived back at the camp feeling absolutely exhausted and so dispirited that we felt like lying down to die. Instead we were pushed downstairs to a large cellar under the original bar. I'm sure that the sound of the other prisoners cheering did nothing to improve the tempers of the Germans and after a few minutes two guards and the camp Commandant came down the stairs. The Commandant was carrying a large bull whip with which he started to hit us. We did our best to protect our heads and faces with our arms until finally, when we thought we were going to die there, the Commandant appeared to be exhausted himself and he suddenly left with the guards, turning off the lights and slamming the trapdoor shut behind him.

Our attempts to protect ourselves had to a large extent been successful in saving our faces, but our arms and backs were very sore and painful. We later agreed that the Commandant seemed to have had a few drinks and had lost his temper so his arm was not as good as it might have been and he had not inflicted as much pain and damage as he might have done, nevertheless, we thought it was bad enough.

After a while and in spite of the pain we did fall asleep through sheer exhaustion but it seemed as though we had hardly closed our eyes before the trapdoor banged open.

Two guards came down the steps and prodded us with their rifles, shouting for us to get upstairs where they pushed us into the back garden to join the rest of the prisoners for roll-call. When we appeared in the garden all the prisoners began cheering and shouting encouragement to us but this only served to make the Commandant very angry.

Through his interpreter the Commandant told all the prisoners that he had taught us a small lesson but because he was a humane and good man he wouldn't have us shot. But if any other prisoner was foolish enough to copy us and make an attempt to escape they would not be so lucky and would be shot immediately. He then went on to say, 'Because I am a generous man I will allow these foolish men to stay in camp today but my generosity is not sufficient to allow me to give them any food until they are fit enough to go out and work for it.

The four of us had to remain standing whilst the remainder of the prisoners, except for those who had duties in the camp and two others who were too sick to work, marched off to work. We were then allowed to return to our bunks and I managed to climb up to mine and then collapsed.

I went to sleep immediately but any thoughts that the Commandant's generosity would allow us to sleep all day was rudely dispelled when, after about an hour, I was awakened by shouting and the prodding of a rifle butt in my ribs. The German guards kept pushing and shouting at me until I nearly fell off the bunk and then I went to the other end of the room and was joined by the other escapees.

We were given brooms and buckets with a small piece of cloth and told to thoroughly clean through every room in the camp on our side of the wire (but for some reason they would not allow us to go through into the kitchen or the German quarters). Although I had enjoyed my short sleep my arms and back still felt very sore and every movement was very painful.

All the cleaning work did nothing to improve my health or feelings as the guards made sure we kept working all the time until about a quarter of an hour before the other prisoners returned to the camp, by which time I could hardly stand let alone keep on sweeping and scrubbing the floors. The other prisoners came in and immediately crowded round our bunks and asked questions about what we had been doing all day and then, more important, they wanted full information about our escapade and full details of the surrounding area and how far we had got before being recaptured.

It was time for ration issue and to ensure that the four of us did not get any food the Commandant had posted an extra guard to watch out for us and he also had to count the rations as they were issued to make sure that only enough for the prisoner strength less four came out of the kitchen. Certainly nobody got any seconds that day but several of the chaps gave us a spoonful of soup so at least we got something.

Because of the wintry weather it was impossible to work on the building site on top of Stolzenberg, and all the prisoners were detailed for other work which could be carried out regardless of the weather with its freezing temperatures and icy winds.

The following day we were detailed to go out on a working party and it was apparent that the guards had received special instructions to keep an extra eye on the four of us and to make absolutely certain that we were kept working which meant no respite whatsoever from the work. On this day we were unlucky enough, or maybe the Commandant had arranged it on purpose, to be detailed to a working party which had to go to a timber yard which stretched for about a hundred yards along a river bank.

The work was very dangerous and involved unloading timber, mainly large pit props, from barges moored alongside jetties and then carrying them for some distance into the timber yard and stacking them. Since the ground and timber was covered with snow and ice it was very difficult to keep a grip on the props and at the same time keep our balance on the treacherous ground. Although there were usually four prisoners carrying each prop the terrible conditions caused several accidents. The injuries were mostly of a minor nature but during the course of a few weeks there were some broken arms and legs.

Gradually the bruises and soreness from the whipping began to fade and our escapade was no longer the main topic of conversation which had again turned to news of the continuing Allied shipping losses which was terribly depressing for us. We longed for some good news for a change, but despite our attempts to change we were still working in the timber yard and considered to be lucky because we had managed to avoid any serious injuries.

Although we had no great desire to go digging trenches, or in fact for any work in Germany, we were all longing for the better weather to come so that we could get back to the safety and comparative peace of the building site on Stolzenberg and of course we would feel warm again instead of perpetually being cold.

Our first Christmas in captivity arrived and the big hearted Germans gave us a day off work and in fact they thought they were being really kind hearted by giving us an extra bowl of watery soup.

Later that evening we could hear the Germans obviously getting drunk and singing loudly in their quarters so some of the lads managed to scrounge a few large empty jam tins, not that we had seen any of the contents I hasten to add, and with these unusual instruments an improvised band was set up to accompany our carol singing. None of us really felt like singing but we thought it would be a good idea to let the Germans know that we could sing, in any case it was much better for us than just sitting around feeling sorry for ourselves and getting even more depressed and homesick.

After singing all the carols that anyone could remember we started on all the old army favourites to be followed by patriotic songs including the National Anthem to let the Germans know that our spirits were still high and we were confident that the Allies would win in the end no matter what the cost or how long it took.

The patriotic songs upset the Germans, some of whom were apparently still sober because the interpreter with a couple of guards came in and told us that we must not sing the National Anthem or any other patriotic songs but they would allow carols.

This announcement was naturally greeted by a lot of jeering and rude and vulgar comments and as the guards turned round and left they had sarcastic shouts of 'Merry Christmas' ringing in their ears. The worst Christmas I had ever had in my life ended with all of us singing 'There'll always be an England' and then we finished off with the National Anthem.

I went to my bunk and lay awake for hours thinking of home and worrying about my mother who was living alone and as far as I was aware she still did not know that I was a prisoner of war.

Chapter 8

Air Raid on Danzig

After Christmas it was a return to the soul-destroying routine of unloading timber in the most miserable and dangerous conditions and in temperatures which dropped to thirty-five degrees Fahrenheit below freezing.[1] In fact it was so cold that the river was frozen solid from bank to bank which was good news since it meant that no barges could be brought along the river to the jetties.

This delay turned out to be of small benefit to us however because when the barges already docked were empty we were put to work re-stacking all the pit props already stacked in the yard. In addition to this we were made to transfer stacks of props from the riverside edge of the timber yard to the other end of the yard which meant we had to carry all the props about a hundred yards. Naturally we thought that all this movement of props was unnecessary and was just seen by the Germans as a way to keep us busy.

No medical facilities were available in our camp which meant that any prisoners requiring medical or dental treatment reported sick and were marched about three miles to an old army barracks which was being used to house a large number of prisoners of many other nationalities but mostly they were French.

---

[1]Equivalent to -19°C.

I was unlucky enough to get severe toothache and despite putting it off for as long as I could, there came a Thursday night when the pain became unbearable and kept me awake all night. Unable to stand the excruciating pain any longer I had to give in and report sick on that Friday morning so I was told to join the sick detail and marched off to the old barracks.

I was sent into a room to wait and eventually in another room I was confronted by the dentist who was known to all prisoners as the Belgian Butcher and I can honestly vouch for that being a very appropriate nickname. Whether he had any qualifications as a dentist I do not know but since he was the only one who was practising and available we didn't have any choice anyway. I sat down on an ordinary kitchen chair which served as his dentist's chair and after he had examined my teeth he decided there was no alternative but to extract the offending tooth.

The Belgian Butcher then proceeded to carry out the extraction whilst two very large chaps struggled to hold me down. As far as I can remember there was no luxury such as an anaesthetic, or if there had been it didn't work and the two chaps really had their work cut out to keep me in the room never mind on the chair. Finally the torture finished and the chaps let me go but I was in such agony that I forgot that I had promised myself that I would take a swipe at the Butcher and left the room just as another poor victim went past me on his way into the torture chamber.

I walked back to camp with the rest of the sick detail clutching my face in terrible agony and trying to convince myself that now the offending tooth had been taken out the excruciating pain would soon stop.

How wrong I was, because the pain continued all through the weekend, which meant I had no sleep and obviously as there were no painkillers available I could not relieve the pain at all, so I seemed to spend all the weekend prowling round the camp. On Monday morning I reported sick again and was escorted back to the old barracks for another face-to-face session with the man I dreaded meeting and hated more than any other person.

I would quite cheerfully have killed him but told myself that I had to wait until he had given me more treatment to relieve the terrible pain in my mouth. Apparently on my first visit he had broken my tooth and left a large piece of it together with the root in my gum. As I sat on the kitchen chair again I was trying to take my mind off the pain and the treatment to come by thinking of how I could get my revenge on the Belgian Butcher. (If the opportunity ever arose I would definitely take it even if it meant murdering him.)

I was again restrained by the two men and after what seemed like an endless struggle, the Butcher succeeded in extracting the remainder of the tooth and the root and I was escorted back to the camp. I managed to scrounge some salt from the kitchen which I used to frequently wash out my mouth but it was several weeks before the pain finally went. Although the actual pain had gone the memory of those visits to the Belgian Butcher and my hatred of him will remain with me for ever but unfortunately I still have not had any opportunity for revenge.

Spring and better weather came after what had seemed like an endless winter, and with the improvement in the weather came the resumption of our routine of walking up the hill to the building site on Stolzenberg. We quickly got back into the routine of digging trenches and laying foundations or drain pipes and desperately trying to avoid doing too much work although, if the truth were known, it was probably much harder to keep on dodging work than doing it in the first place. We did, however, get immense satisfaction from the knowledge that it must be the slowest building project ever and the thought that we were putting one over the Germans gave us a boost.

We heard over the grapevine that HMS Hood had been sunk and that the blitz on London was continuing unabated. Also about this time we heard of the weird flight of Hess to Scotland. A lot of our information came from the Polish civilians who were working on the site and at about the end of June they told us about the invasion of Russia.

It was shortly after this that the German guards started boasting about the marvellous Wehrmacht who were unstoppable just overrunning the Russians in the same way that they had gone through the Low Countries and France. All this bad news was making us very despondent and we began wondering how, when and where it would be possible to stop this apparently invincible German army. Strangely, despite all the bad news and against all the odds, it was still our belief that ultimately Britain and her Allies would emerge victorious.

Gradually the conditions under which we lived began to improve and later in the summer we began to receive mail from home. My mother told me that she had thought I had been killed in action until September 1940, about four months after my capture when she had been officially notified that I was alive and a prisoner of war.
The German guards continued to derive great pleasure from telling us about the rapid advances that the Wehrmacht were making on the Russian Front, and increasingly now about their marvellous U-Boats and the huge losses they, were inflicting on Allied shipping. We also heard about the fierce fighting taking place around Tobruk in Africa so it seemed that nothing was going right for the Allies.

One evening we received our rations of bread and soup as usual and then were told to parade in the back garden. Word went round like wildfire that at last some more Red

The following letter was received by Major - General Sir John Davidson, K.C.M.G., C.B., D.S.O., Colonel Commandant 2nd Battalion, The King's Royal Rifle Corps, from the Private Secretary to H.M. The King :—

BUCKINGHAM PALACE.

5th June, 1940.

My dear General,

The King, as Colonel-in-Chief of The King's Royal Rifle Corps, has learned with pride of the heroic action of the 2nd Battalion and The Queen Victoria's Rifles at Calais, which assisted so materially in the successful evacuation of the British Expeditionary Force. Such self-sacrifice and gallantry are in keeping with the highest traditions of his Majesty's Regiment and mark a glorious page in its history.

I am desired to assure you of the heartfelt sympathy of the Colonel-in- Chief with the relatives of all ranks of these two Battalions in the great anxiety through which they are passing.

Yours very sincerely,
(Signed) Alexander Hardinge

The letter my mother received in September 1940.

Cross parcels had arrived but in fact the number of parcels were so few again that the amount each prisoner received was very small. I received a teaspoonful of jam and a spoonful of sardine, which although a small meal certainly tasted very different from our usual fare. We also received a tin of condensed milk to be shared between five of us which gave us a problem in calculating shares but did give us a lovely addition to the meal.

In the autumn we started to get more parcels through the International Red Cross which included items of clothing. It must be an undisputed fact that the Red Cross parcels saved the lives and minds of many prisoners, because if we had continued to struggle to exist on German rations alone there would have been many deaths from malnutrition and the lack of proper hygiene.

Our monotonous routine of going to the building site on Stolzenberg continued uneventfully until one evening when we were in the back garden queuing for our rations we heard the sound of aircraft. There were the usual cries of, 'Don't worry they're ours', and Nobby Clark said, Blimey they really are ours – they're Lancasters'. At this moment the air raid sirens started wailing and the German guards were going mad shouting and trying to push us into the building. We tried to resist because we wanted to watch the aircraft and at the same time, were cheering and telling the guards, 'Now you're going to get some stick! Wait for the bombs – here they come!'

At long last the German guards succeeded in getting all the prisoners back into the building and although it was almost dark by this time, everybody made a dash to get near the small windows so that they could watch all the excitement.

The ones who managed to get a good viewpoint were giving a running commentary and said the sky was lit by searchlights scanning the whole area for the aircraft. We could hear bombs falling and the sound of heavy anti-aircraft fire. A voice said, 'I hope the silly buggers don't drop a bomb on us' and someone replied, 'It's worth any risk just to hear the bombs falling on the German bastards. As far as I am concerned it's music in my ears and the longer it goes on and the more they drop the better'. After quite a long time the raiders departed and the all-clear sounded but the sky remained lit by a red glow, presumably from fires started by incendiary bombs. This raid was a really big boost to our morale and everyone discussed it for hours after the usual lights-out time.

The only regret we had was that the timing was wrong because it meant we did not get any rations that night and we all wished that the Lancasters had dropped a load of Red Cross parcels in the back garden to compensate us for the missed rations.

The next morning we were very surprised to see that the number of guards was double our usual escort and when we went out of the front door we were greeted by shouts, waving fists and stones thrown by some of the crowd. From this reception we understood why the guards had been doubled but still did not know the reason for the sudden outburst of hatred.

Later we learned that some of the bombs had landed on a children's hospital killing some of the young patients and this tragedy obviously accounted for the extra guards and the anger of the crowd. Although we fully understood their feelings we believed that most of the blame for the tragedy should fall on the Germans themselves because they had located the hospital next door to their Area Military Headquarters.

Knowing the Germans as we did, we thought it was possible that the positioning of the hospital and the head-quarters had been deliberate in the hope that the Allied intelligence service would advise the RAF not to bomb that area. Alternatively if it was bombed it would provide useful propaganda (it did of course).

The death of innocent children made us feel very sad as did the fact that a Lancaster had been brought down with no survivors. It was a very sad day when some prisoners from our camp had to march to a nearby cemetery and carry the coffins containing the crew of the Lancaster from army trucks into a small chapel for a short service and then to the graves where they formed a guard of honour.

After some time the memories of the incident began to fade and life went on with the usual boring routine, until one evening when we heard over the grapevine that the Japanese had carried out an unprovoked attack on the Americans at Pearl Harbor and the news that this cowardly attack had resulted in the Americans at last joining in the war. The general opinion was that as usual the Americans had been a bit slow in starting but we were cheered now by the fact that at last we would be getting some help.

Unfortunately it was also about this time that we heard of the sinking of the Prince of Wales and the Repulse, news which at first we found very hard to believe but after confirmation from various sources we had to accept as fact. The weather was gradually getting more wintry again and eventually it was time for us to stop working on the building site on Stolzenberg and to be detailed for different working parties for the winter months.

I was praying that I would avoid the timber yard this year and I believe someone must have been listening to my prayers because they were answered. I was detailed to a working party of twenty prisoners and marched along Friedrichstrasse to the main railway station. In the main road in front of the station we were told to climb on to a streetcar (similar to a tram but consisting of two carriages with a large platform between them) which ran along tracks in the road. No prisoners were allowed to sit down or mingle with other passengers so we had to squeeze together and stay standing on the platform for the half-hour journey.

When we arrived at our stop we were encouraged to get off by the guards doing their usual act of prodding us with their rifles and once lined up in some semblance of order we had to march along the road, until to our great astonishment and delight we arrived at a brewery. Once inside the yard four prisoners were detailed to go with horses and carts which were driven by Polish civilians down to the nearby river which was completely frozen over. They then had an awful job of cutting blocks of ice out of the river and loading them on to the carts which when full were driven back to the brewery.

When the carts got back, the rest of the working party had to unload them and stack the blocks of ice in a huge barn-like building. We soon discovered that there were a large number of Polish women working in a bottling shed on the other side of the yard, and from then on the German guards had their work cut out trying to prevent us from joining them.

By now we were very experienced at scrounging and smuggling goods into the camp and I regularly took in eight bottles of beer with one down each leg, held in by string tied round my trousers at my ankle, four under my clothing behind my back and two more held in front by a string belt.

I shall never forget one morning when we were standing on the streetcar platform and as usual cursing all and sundry in typical army fashion with practically every other word a swear word, when to our amazement the conductress in a broad Geordie accent, told us to watch our language as there was a lady present.

When we had recovered from the shock we learnt that she was from Newcastle and had married a Danziger in early 1938 and been trapped for the duration but naturally she was not broadcasting details of her place of birth for fear of imprisonment or worse, but when she heard us talking in English she had been unable to resist the temptation to speak in English for the first time for years.

We hoped our little chat cheered her up but we feared it may have made her homesick, although of course she had chosen to live in her husband's homeland and until the outbreak of war had loved her life in Danzig even if she hated it now. We said goodbye to her with a Geordie prisoner saying it in a typical accent from Tyneside and we could see she had tears in her eyes when we left the streetcar and marched off down the road to the brewery.

Unfortunately this dream job only lasted for three weeks but even in that short time we had succeeded in smuggling a surprisingly large number of bottles of beer in to the camp for Christmas.

This Christmas was a big improvement on the last one because of the supply of Red Cross parcels plus some others from home which meant there was a vast improvement in the amount and quality of food and of course in our clothing.

A new orchestra was formed with instruments which were received from the International Red Cross – two clarinets, a guitar, flute, violin, drums, trumpet, trombone and three accordions – and they gave us a marvellous concert. Of course even I had to admit that their accompaniment to our carol singing was a vast improvement on the old jam tins. But in spite of all this and all our attempts to be cheerful we still felt depressed and thought continually about home and loved ones and the course of the war. We were so longing for it to end so that we could go home.

Chapter 9

Building a New Camp

After Christmas the same depressing routine of outside working parties continued. I was feeling even more depressed than usual because we no longer had the relatively cheerful job at the brewery to look forward to and instead I landed a job clearing old rubbish out of some warehouses and then repainting all the inside walls and ceilings.

We did our best to waste the paint and generally make a lousy job of it. We were still annoyed because there was nothing worth scrounging and there were no girls to liven up proceedings as there had been at the brewery which had raised our hopes falsely.

When the weather had improved sufficiently we again resumed the trek up the hill to Stolzenberg. The guards were still apparently getting great enjoyment from telling us about the marvellous Wehrmacht and their continuing victories in Russia. They also enjoyed telling us about the invincible U-Boats which were still causing huge Allied shipping losses in the Atlantic. But then we heard over the grapevine that the Germans had been forced to retreat from Moscow.

At about this time we also heard about the Japanese attack in Malaya and we were longing to hear some really good news, in particular a great British victory on sea or land anywhere in the world but preferably against the

Germans so that we could shut the guards up when they were going on about the damned Wehrmacht.

A large party of prisoners was put to work on a big area on the edge of the Stolzenberg building site and we discovered that it was preparation for a new and much larger camp which was going to be built for us, presumably because of the overcrowding in the old Beer Garden premises – although knowing the German mentality it could have been just to save time by having the prisoners housed on top of the site.

Nobby said, 'If those bloody Germans think the time saved from not walking up the hill will mean I'll be able to dig another six foot of trench they're going to be bloody unlucky. I'm more likely to turn stroppy and try even harder to do less – if that's possible. All the prisoners were hired out to a firm of building contractors who paid the Wehrmacht for the guards, our labour and all the running expenses of the camp including food. (The amount of food given to prisoners couldn't have shown up as a very large amount in the accounts unless somebody was fiddling and making a huge profit.)

The intention was for the prisoners, together with the Polish civilians working under German overseers, to build a huge estate comprised of many blocks of flats, three storeys high. We were promised payment for our work in Lagergeldt (specially printed money for prisoners of war). In theory we would then be able to exchange the Lagergeldt for all types of goods but in practice it turned out that if we were very lucky we would get some very rough Polish tobacco and cigarette papers or cigarettes which were two-thirds cardboard. However, on one or two occasions we did actually get some razor blades.

It was at about this time that the guards were getting great pleasure out of regaling us with tales of the marvellous victories being won by their hero Rommel and the Afrika Korps.

Then we heard over the grapevine that Singapore had fallen to the Japanese, but some of the old soldiers who had served in Singapore refused to believe the story and maintained it must be propaganda because they thought that Singapore was impregnable. We also heard from the same source that a few weeks previously the bitter freezing weather and fierce attacks by Russian troops had forced the German Army to retreat.

Although we had the story confirmed by a friendly Polish civilian it was very difficult to get up to date news from the Russian Front and certainly the Germans would do their utmost to prevent any adverse news getting through their usual propaganda.

When the new camp was completed it consisted of five single-storey wooden huts each about two hundred feet long. The first three were divided into rooms in the following sequence. Firstly a room approximately twenty foot square with twelve sets of double bunks against the walls round the room and in the centre a large round iron stove. Adjoining this room was one of similar size but containing tables and benches to be shared with the occupants of the other room also containing twelve sets of bunks. The entrance to each set of three rooms was through a main door in the communal leisure/dining room.

This sequence of rooms was repeated three times which meant that each hut had six dormitory rooms and three dining rooms so that the maximum capacity was one hundred and forty-four prisoners in each hut. The fourth hut was of the same length and contained toilets, showers, officer and warrant officer accommodation and a sick bay whilst the fifth hut contained a kitchen, storerooms and a large concert/recreation hall.

Between each hut were air raid shelters which ran the complete length of the huts and had been constructed by digging a trench about six feet deep, placing old railway sleepers across the top for a roof and then covering the lot with the earth that had been dug from the trench which in due course became covered with grass.

The whole complex was surrounded by two high wire fences with a double row of barbed wire along the top and these fences were separated by a gap of about three feet. At each corner there were watch-towers continually manned by guards with machine guns. Outside the main gate was a sentry box permanently manned by a guard and also outside the camp was another long hut which contained the accommodation for the Germans.

Chapter 10

Third Christmas

The historic day came when we left the old Beer Garden for the last time but I don't think any prisoner really regretted leaving. We went marching down Friedrichstrasse carrying all our worldly possessions, (mine were in my pockets).

As we went past the children's hospital which still bore the scars of the bombing it brought back sad memories of the air crew and children who had been killed. Next to it was the Military Headquarters with no visible signs of any bombing at which several of us were shouting vulgar comments about their lack of fathers and giving a good version of an alternative victory salute.

When we were going past the railway station we realised that our destination was probably the de-lousing station and it turned out to be an accurate guess. On our arrival we had to go through the same procedure of being completely shaved, then going through the showers and of course coming out at the end to receive back our clothes still damp and stinking of chemicals.

Our return journey took us back along Friedrichstrasse straight past the old Beer Garden and up the hill to Stolzenberg to enter the new camp for the first time. Of course at each stage we had suffered the usual delays while the Germans carried out their counts but after a final count we were allowed through the gates into the camp in groups of twenty-four and directed to one of the dormitories.

I was directed to the second room of the hut next to the perimeter fences which was farthest from the main gate and the Germans but unfortunately, also furthest from the kitchen, toilets and showers. After claiming a bunk and settling in, several of us went wandering round the camp inspecting the showers and washbasins which to our amazement were fed with hot water for washing ourselves and our clothes.

We thought we were in paradise (except that there were no girls in grass skirts) and it really was paradise when you compare it with other camps we had been in and had heard about.

The only problem was that at night all the main doors were locked which meant that the only toilet facilities available during the night was a large oil drum which stood in the corner of the dining/leisure room for the use of forty-eight men. As a result of this arrangement there had to be a roster for the unpleasant task of carrying the oil drum for about forty yards to dispose of the contents in the toilet drains every morning.

On the same day that we arrived another party of prisoners arrived from the Stalag headquarters at Marienburg to make up the full complement of the camp and with this party there was a medical officer who was a major in the RAMC and a warrant officer from the Ox and Bucks.

Doug a Scot from Glasgow, said, 'If they think they are going to instil discipline in this camp they're in for a nasty shock, although I don't mind the doctor because he may let us have some more days off.' Conditions generally began to improve and we started to get more regular supplies of Red Cross parcels and also more mail and clothing parcels from home. The improvement particularly in the food and tobacco situation brought about a steady increase in morale and every day became a contest to see who could cause the most problems for the Germans, and especially who could do the least amount of work. We heard about the commando raid at St Nazaire which brought back memories to those us who had fought and been captured in that area in 1940. We also heard the bad news of Japanese atrocities and stories of the fierce fighting on the Russian Front.

Most of us had become experts at scrounging all sorts of items including food which made life a little easier, and from an economic and convenience point of view it became general practice to form small groups to share food and chores because, for example, it was much more sensible for a group to share a tin of meat for one meal than for an individual to use a tin over a period of days.

The group I was in consisted of Tiny Carr, a regular soldier from Yorkshire, Yorkie Thomas who had been a prisoner of war in the Great War and who was obviously also a Yorkshireman, Jack Guthrie from Dundee, Jim McDonald from Glasgow and myself, a Londoner.

By this time we were mostly preparing our own meals on the big iron stove in the centre of the room and only drawing rations from the kitchen merely to use up the German supplies although if we got any potatoes they were added to our meals.

Most of that summer was spent levelling ground and digging trenches for foundations and main drainage pipes although some prisoners were already working with civilians in laying foundations and actually building a wall. But as usual the work was proceeding at a snail's pace.

The evenings were spent rehearsing with the newly formed Concert Party or listening to concerts given by the camp orchestra. There were also numerous other activities such as various sports, language classes (chiefly German) and painting classes.

We were getting news about the RAF's bombing raids on cities like Cologne, the German advances on the Russian Front again, the seemingly all-conquering Japanese in Burma, rumours that Heydrich had been assassinated, details of Rommel's successes in Africa and the fall of Tobruk, and of course the inevitable stories of huge Allied shipping losses. Overall the news gave us nothing to be cheerful about.

In the autumn we heard about the commando raid on Dieppe and we got some idea of the German anger it caused when they made us leave our boots and trousers in the concert hall every night as some form of reprisal. This action lasted a few nights because every morning the prisoners were deliberately taking a very long time to find their own boots and trousers which resulted in the prisoners being very slow to get into their working parties and this made the Germans change their minds and stop the stupid practice.

The snow came and with it bitterly cold weather which meant, as usual, that work stopped on the building site and all the prisoners were allocated to small working parties and dispersed round the surrounding area.

Fortunately I again managed to avoid the terrible timber yard but although the job I was allocated to was much safer it was soul destroying because of the utter boredom. We had to use various tools such as pickaxes, shovels and a tool similar to a garden hoe to clear ice from the pavements and shovel it into the gutter to await collection or be left to melt.

We used to have daily competitions to see who could clear the smallest space and the winner usually kept his clearance down to about a square yard, but often it was impossible to decide. Our biggest problem, apart from convincing the Germans we were working hard, was to keep warm and with us stamping our feet in practically the same spot for hours on end I cannot understand why we did not wear a hole in the pavement.

One of our greatest pleasures was making nasty remarks or swearing at the civilians and soldiers who passed by. Our attempts to accidentally trip them up were often hilarious and if one of us succeeded in making anyone stumble or fall down it was a real high spot of the day. This explanation should illustrate the utter boredom we were feeling that such stupid activities gave such a lot of pleasure. The French prisoners were allowed to walk around the town unaccompanied and as I said before there was no love lost between the British and the French. So it was hardly surprising when two men walked by looking like French prisoners that I said to Jock, 'There goes some more of those Froggie bastards'. We were both dumbstruck when a few moments later they returned and as they went by, one said, 'Not so much of the Froggie bastards, we're the RAF'.

This meeting really provided a talking point when we returned to the camp that night and we all wished them the best of luck and wondered how far they would get.

The Germans issued a newspaper specially printed for prisoners of war called *Camp* which naturally contained a considerable amount of propaganda but unfortunately a lot of the stories especially about the huge shipping tonnage that the U-Boats were sinking in the Atlantic which turned out to be true. But the other main stories referring to the Wehrmacht's continued advance on the Russian Front and that Rommel and his Afrika Korps was conquering all in North Africa were still stretching the truth a bit to put it politely. We heard over the grapevine that Montgomery and the Eighth Army had been successful at El Alamein and also that the Russians were putting up a very strong resistance around Stalingrad, and this news did cheer us up a little bit.

The dreary routine of going out on working parties continued but in the evenings a large number of prisoners were fully occupied in rehearsals for the forthcoming Christmas pantomime whilst others worked hard as scenery painters and costume makers, improvising with all sorts of materials which had been scrounged, bought or bartered for.

Naturally because it was an all-male preserve and had been for a long time there were a large number of candidates for the role of principal boy. In fact, it caused quite a lot of jealousy amongst those of the prisoners who were that way inclined.

Christmas 1942, our third one in captivity, came and the pantomime was a huge success making all the hard work worthwhile. The fact that we had sufficient food and cigarettes went a long way towards making it better than previous years although there was a sad lack of drinks.

My group only managed to get a bottle of schnapps and a couple of bottles of beer which was obviously not enough for us to drown our sorrows and the feelings of homesickness. We had the usual singing of carols, patriotic and other popular songs but to some extent this only served to make most of the prisoners long for home even more and particularly affected all those who had families with young children.

All of us were constantly hoping and praying for some really good news and of course above everything else was the hope that 1943 would be the year when the war ended and we could all return home. Amazingly in view of the fact that for all the time we had spent in captivity we had been bombarded with bad news we still remained firmly convinced that the Germans would be defeated.

We continued with our boring job of clearing the snow and ice from the pavements but now that Christmas was over there was a feeling of anticlimax and without any pantomime to spend time rehearsing for, the atmosphere became very depressing. However in a few weeks the camp Orchestra began giving concerts again and several prisoners started rehearsing for a play, so there were many prisoners occupied and entertained which all helped to lift the clouds of depression.

Chapter 11

Improving Our Environment

Spring was arriving and the weather was gradually improving so that we could again return to working on the building site. It was not long after this start that the first block of flats was nearing completion and I was working with a group of Polish workmen as a carpenter fixing roof joists and purlins.

The carpentry work definitely did not appeal to me very much because I am really scared of heights although I stuck at it for several weeks. At the first opportunity I miraculously became a qualified bricklayer although, if the truth were told, I picked up the rudiments of bricklaying as I went along with the help of a couple of friends who really were proficient bricklayers. The Camp newspaper continued to regale us with stories of the marvellous victories being achieved by the invincible German forces but we were really pleased to hear about the Eighth Army's advances and the success of the Russians at Stalingrad with the amazing news of the surrender of General Paulus and so many of his troops. Needless to say, we did not get that news from the Camp newspaper but through the secretive grapevine source.

We did become proficient at reading between the lines in the Camp newspaper and it became evident that even in that publication the number of successes were growing less and the claims were not so extravagant as they used to be.

Work on the building site continued and as the buildings progressed towards completion so the deliveries of electric wiring, plugs, ovens and ceramic tiles began to arrive. These deliveries were greatly appreciated by the prisoners who immediately started to steal and smuggle large quantities of the various items into the camp and in practically no time at all they were being used to transform our rooms. In fact our entire environment was dramatically changed for the better.

The large iron stove in the centre of every dormitory room was converted by adding a brick oven behind it faced with some nice ceramic tiles and having a square metal oven from the inside of an electric cooker inside it. The heat was supplied by running the chimney from the original stove around the metal oven inside the brick and tile construction and then up to the roof and out through the original aperture.

This modification enabled us to make a much greater variety of menus from the Red Cross parcels and the inventiveness of the amateur chefs was truly remarkable although, I must say, on a few occasions the end result did have an unusual taste to say the least. Nevertheless it all had to be eaten because in our circumstances it would have been sacrilege to waste any food.

As well as all the electrical equipment used for modifications in the dormitories a considerable amount of supplies found their way into the Concert Hall and was used to make every kind of lighting system that could be devised, and some knowledgeable people considered the equipment and system compared favourably with the facilities of many West End theatres back in London.

One Sunday morning I was playing our form of netball which was a mixture of netball and rugby, certainly it was no game for the weak or squeamish. As my plimsolls kept slipping off I discarded them and continued playing in my bare feet when suddenly Jack Thomas, a big Welsh Guardsman jumped to tackle me and as he came down he landed with his size ten boots on my big toe. I almost fainted with the pain and although Jack was very apologetic that didn't stop me from telling him in some vile army language exactly what I thought of him and his ancestry.

There was quite a lot of blood pouring from my toe which looked a real mess so a couple of the chaps carried me down to the sick bay and the Medical Officer was brought from his quarters. The doctor examined my toe and decided he would have to give me a general anaesthetic so that he could cut out the smashed toenail and put in a few stitches. The small operating theatre was got ready by the Medical Orderly and the doctor then carried out the small operation. As far as I am concerned the only good thing about this accident was that I had to stay in the sick bay for a few days and was excused work for a week.

I should explain that the sick bay in the camp was like a small hospital and was fully equipped although of course some drugs and medicines were in short supply. The Medical Officer was a Major in the RAMC and was responsible for the health and welfare of British prisoners of war in a large area surrounding Danzig. Prisoners from the other camps used to come regularly to our camp for treatment.

It was about a week after my operation that quite by chance I overheard the Medical Orderly talking to a couple of chaps and telling them that I was very lucky to be alive because apparently when I was under the anaesthetic I appeared to have died. Fortunately for me the Medical Officer had acted very promptly and succeeded in reviving me although there were to be many occasions in the future when I woke up and wondered whether he had in fact done me a favour.

After a week of rest my toe had healed quite well and I was judged to be fit enough to resume work on the building site.

The first blocks of flats were completed and soon there were gas-driven trucks and horse and carts arriving laden with furniture and household goods which marked the arrival of the first families to have the dubious pleasure of living in flats constructed by prisoner labour.

Gradually as time passed we were becoming resigned to life in a prison camp. We were becoming contemptuous and almost patronising towards the German guards and our attitude undoubtedly upset some of them but we ignored any sort of reaction from them.

We were still getting regular issues of the Camp newspaper which still inevitably contained details of glorious German victories and we had become very good at interpreting the true meaning. For instance, we knew that if it said that the Wehrmacht had halted for a short rest before a final onslaught we knew that in fact they were retreating and the stories we had heard over the grapevine confirmed that the tide was turning on the Russian Front.

At roll-call one morning all Irishmen were told to report to the concert hall and we discovered afterwards that a German officer had given a lecture telling them that Germany and Ireland were not at war, but, in fact, very friendly and there was no need for them to remain as prisoners of war.

Apparently a couple of the Irishmen fell for this story and were immediately taken from the camp and it wasn't until about three weeks later that one of them returned to the camp and told us what had happened to him after he had left the concert hall.

It appears that this lecture bad been given to Irishmen at all the prison camps containing British prisoners of war and quite a large number of Irishmen had believed the story and been taken to Berlin and when they arrived they had been given good meals, taken out round the night clubs and generally made a real fuss of.

After a few days of this conditioning they were all asked to join a special battalion of foreigners which was being formed to fight with the Germans against the Russians. Our informant could not tell us if many, or indeed if any, had fallen for it and joined but he said as far as he was concerned he had had a marvellous holiday in Berlin. He told the Germans he had already seen enough ice and snow without going to Russia but had not made up his mind yet and wanted a little more time to think about it.

Although the Germans were getting a bit cross about it they were still trying to persuade him to join but he was very insistent that he must have more time to think and reluctantly they had let him return to the camp on the understanding that he would definitely think about joining their foreign battalion and try and get others in the camp to join with him – apparently they didn't mind whether any new recruits were Irish or any other nationality.

Shortly after this episode we had several German officers visit the camp and they were accompanied by another chap in German uniform whose shoulder badge read 'Britische Freikorps'. We very soon discovered he was an Australian who had been taken prisoner in Crete and that the main purpose of his visit was to encourage as many Allied prisoners of war as possible to join this newly formed unit to go and fight alongside the Germans against the Russians.

When this became obvious the prisoners were furious and several made threatening moves towards the Australian, calling him some unprintable names and telling him in no uncertain terms exactly what they would do to him when they got hold of him. The Germans saw the prisoners' reaction and became very agitated so that the guards had to fix bayonets and more or less keep the prisoners at bay whilst the German officers and the Australian beat a hasty retreat out of the camp.

There were plenty of stories circulating after this visit about how many prisoners had been persuaded to join the Freikorps and the numbers we heard varied from fifty to five hundred and although I never did find out the true figure I know for certain that there were no volunteers from our camp.

By this time several of the guards were wounded veterans from the Russian Front and one in particular used to spend nearly all his lunch break in the small wooden hut with us while we had our lunch, regaling us with stories of his bravery and how he had single-handedly destroyed several Russian tanks.

We had tried everything we could think of to shut him up but without success until one of the lads had a bright idea and said he would have a word with Johnny Nicholls to see if he would help which everybody agreed was worth a try.

Johnny Nicholls was a big Guardsman who had been awarded the Victoria Cross 'posthumously' for wiping out a German machine gun post in France in 1940.

When it subsequently came to light that he was a prisoner of war the International Red Cross had sent him magazines which contained pictures of his wife dressed in mourning attending Buckingham Palace to receive his Victoria Cross.

The Germans had of course been told of his award by the Red Cross and one morning when the prisoners were lined up for roll-call the German Commandant strode on to the parade ground and called Johnny Nicholls to the front and told him that the Germans admired bravery and as a mark of their admiration for him he could have anything he wanted (except his freedom). So Johnny asked for a brand new pair of boots and a couple of days later these were given to him.

Normally Johnny was excused working parties because he still had terrible bouts of pain in his chest where he had received the most terrible wounds and I can remember one occasion in particular when the pain had been so bad that he had picked up a bench and tossed it through a window which seemed to help relieve the pressure, but certainly did nothing for the bench or the window. Even damage like this was covered up by the Medical Officer who used his influence to clear it with the Commandant.

But to get back to the story of the German guard who was making a nuisance of himself during our lunch breaks. We spoke to Johnny and explained the situation and he agreed to come out with our working party the next day and we went into the hut as usual for lunch which normally consisted of a small sandwich and ersatz coffee. As expected the German guard started telling us of his courageous exploits on the Russian Front.

We signalled to Johnny and made room for him on the bench so that he was sitting directly opposite the German and as the German continued with his stories Johnny just sat there.

Johnny now began moving his face towards the German and gradually the German began to talk slower and slower and his voice was getting quieter until finally, when Johnny's, face was just a few inches from his he stopped talking altogether while Johnny just sat there glaring at him without saying a word. Suddenly the German seemed to lose his nerve and all appetite for storytelling and he jumped up and quickly scampered out of the hut while Johnny and the rest of us burst out laughing. From that moment on we never heard another story from that guard and we noticed he always tried to get with another group if he could to avoid our laughter every time we saw him.

Our sources of news informed us that there had been a slight improvement in the fortunes of the Allies insofar as Rommel and his Afrika Korps, at least what was left of it, had been forced to leave Africa. There was heavy fighting on the Russian Front and large scale bombing raids were being carried out over Germany so this upturn in fortunes cheered us up considerably.

More and more families moved into the flats on the estate and the prisoners, having been starved of female companionship for such a long time and now that food was no longer a great problem, their thoughts turned once again to sex as the most important need. There was quite a lot of competition amongst the prisoners to see who could develop a relationship with one of the women now living in the flats. Quite a few succeeded, sometimes with tragic consequences, but in many cases provided us with some really hilarious moments.

The author prior to going
to France.

The author in 1945.

The Stolzenberg building
site. Author wearing cap
in trench at back.

With Polish carpenters on the building site. Author second from
right.

With fellow prisoners.
Author on right.

Author centre, back row.

The author's service medals.

The author's British army dog tag *(top)* and German prisoner-of-war tag bearing the number 10706.

Chapter 12

Mixing With the Locals

I will always remember one particular occasion when I saw Jack White beating a hasty retreat out of a back window clutching all of his clothes in his arms because the husband had returned home unexpectedly. It was fortunate for Jack that the flat he was hurriedly leaving was on the first floor and not on the third, and of course that no guard had seen him and that as he landed several prisoners stood around him to shield him from any unwelcome eyes.

Another occasion that sticks in my mind was when Tom Jackson decided to disappear with his girlfriend who had been working in the office responsible for issuing passes and had acquired a pass for him. Several weeks later we heard that they had been caught whilst trying to cross the Swiss frontier. Tom could consider himself fortunate as all he got was a short sentence in the cooler but it had probably meant the death sentence for his girlfriend although we were never able to confirm this.

I had arranged to meet one of the tenants in the basement of one of the blocks of flats one morning as the basements were generally considered to be much safer places for clandestine meetings than the actual flats. This particular basement I was in had several lockable rooms for each flat to use for storage. It was about nine o'clock and I was waiting impatiently for the lady to arrive when the door leading upstairs opened and to my horror, instead of the lady I was expecting, a man walked through and looked at me suspiciously.

I think I showed great presence of mind when I immediately started looking on the floor as if I had lost something. By now, like most of the prisoners, I had picked up a fair smattering of German so when he spoke to me in German I realised he was asking me, 'What are you doing here?' I replied, also in German, 'I am looking for my cigarette lighter, I was working down here yesterday and since I could not find my lighter anywhere I thought that I must have dropped it down here but I cannot find it so I had better go,' and I turned round and went through the door leading to the back of the flats. My heart and pulse kept racing for ages and I kept thinking what a narrow escape I had had. When I saw the woman again I discovered that the man who had surprised me in the basement was her husband who had been late leaving for work that morning, so I made a resolution never to make any early-morning arrangements in future.

I was now working as a bricklayer and we were all fully occupied trying to devise methods of making our work substandard and ways of doing as little as possible. Tools and equipment frequently disappeared; in fact some of them were buried in concrete and at some time in the future they may provide archaeologists with some interesting artefacts.

Another popular trick was to concrete over the chimney space and then to quickly carry on building, I imagine this caused a few problems when they first tried to light the fires in the built-in ovens. Another favourite trick was to distract the guards and then the chaps laying the main drainage pipes under what would soon be the main road would drop large boulders on to the pipes to smash them and then quickly cover them with earth.

We were continually trying to establish contacts who could help us in any way to escape and I spent a lot of time chatting with Polish workmen on the estate to find out whether they knew of any helpful contacts or if they had any information which could be useful. They were very frightened and I could understand that, particularly since I knew that one of their workmates had recently been arrested and taken to Treblinka concentration camp but was freed unexpectedly after six months and allowed to return to his work on the estate. I was never able to find out why he received such a lenient sentence and he was the only person the Polish workmen knew of who had ever been released from Treblinka so naturally he was treated with deep suspicion and most of the time he was avoided by the other Poles.

I must admit that I was shocked by his appearance, because when arrested he was in his early twenties but after his release looked more like a man of sixty; his nerves were shattered and he was too scared to talk about his experiences inside Treblinka.

By this time we were busily involved in bartering our Red Cross supplies for food and other items not normally obtainable such as cameras or radios, mostly with the Polish workmen but occasionally with a German guard.

It was normal practice for members of outside working parties to return with eggs on their heads underneath their berets or down their trouser-legs held up by gaiters or maybe they would have bags of sugar suspended by string down between their legs.

Another popular practice was to carry a large farmhouse loaf underneath their battledress blouse at the back which tended to give the impression that the person was carrying a haversack on his back.

There were numerous methods used to distract the gate guard's attention while the working parties hurried through the main gate of the camp but one classic example which always springs to mind was whenever a certain guard who we had discovered was deeply religious was on duty, one of the prisoners would pull out a Bible and start a religious discussion with him while the rest of the working party hurried through the gate.

On a few occasions when a special item was being brought in another prisoner would make sure that the guard found a small article of contraband on him and he would then with the help of other prisoners create as much fuss as possible so that it became a scene of utter chaos; meanwhile of course the prisoner with the important item would quickly slip through the gate. Some of us took dangerous chances and deceived the German guards into giving us food or other items in exchange for a packet of cigarettes when in fact the packet was filled mostly with paper and only had cigarette ends visible when opened. Another trick was to empty a packet of coffee and refill it with ersatz coffee and then cover it with a very thin layer of real coffee on top.

We gambled a lot on the German guards being too scared of the consequences if they were discovered to have dealt with the prisoners and obviously you could not play the same trick on the same guard and you had to be careful to avoid them afterwards.

Although we realised it was a dangerous game to play we did it as often as possible because, apart from getting items we wanted, it gave us so much pleasure to get some revenge on the Germans. There was never any shortage of volunteers willing to take the risk and certainly none of us ever felt any pangs of conscience for being so dishonest.

If any guards, particularly new ones, became too nasty we could invariably take them down a peg or two by threatening to make up stories to tell the Commandant. Usually the guards were so scared of being punished by a posting to the Eastern Front to fight the Russians that they backed down but of course there were one or two exceptions and we had to be very careful which sometimes meant taking several days to determine a guard's character.

Chapter 13

Escape Attempts

I struck up a friendship with a Danziger girl who hated the Germans and one day we were sitting in the restaurant at the main railway station where the attraction was not the food which was nothing to write home about, but rather it was the almost forgotten pleasure of sitting in a restaurant with a very attractive young woman. It brought back memories of happier times in the pre-war days of peace, freedom, normal living and normal behaviour.

We had just finished our meal and were just sitting there enjoying Players cigarettes when I saw the camp Commandant with some other officers entering the restaurant. I was so surprised that a sudden inhalation of smoke had me coughing and spluttering and although on the verge of panicking, with a great effort I managed to control myself.

We waited until the Commandant and his companions moved away from the entrance and had settled down at a table before I signalled to my companion. We got up as casually as possible and walked slowly to the door. My friend paid the cashier while I, keeping my face turned away from the Commandant, went out through the door.

This experience had really shaken us both and made us realise just how dangerous it was to be in public places together, especially confined places like restaurants, so although we continued to meet it was always in more isolated places.

A few weeks later I had another scare and it happened just after I had left her and was returning to the building site by a back footpath when I saw a German guard coming down the hill towards me. I realised that if I suddenly turned and hurried back down the hill it might arouse the guard's suspicion so I decided the only alternative was for me to try and act naturally as if I had every right to be there. As I went past the guard I said, 'Guten Tag', and the guard replied likewise and I just continued up the hill with my heart thumping like mad.

I can only assume he thought I was one of the Polish workmen or maybe one of the new tenants on the estate. Anyway I was very thankful although it was many minutes before my heart and pulse rate got back to normal.

One of the working parties smuggled in a Royal Air Force chap who had escaped from a Luftstalag about fifty miles away. We constructed a hideaway for him in the roof space of our hut and worked out a system for warning him in the event of any Germans prowling around so he could quickly climb up into his hideaway, where he did in fact sleep for most nights for the length of his stay. He was smuggled in and out of the camp quite frequently and apparently used to spend his time trying to contact someone who could help him get on to a Swedish ship. Occasionally he would wander around in the vicinity of the docks to see if there was any way he could get straight on to a Swedish ship without any assistance and he had many narrow escapes because obviously the docks were a very sensitive area and subject to many patrols and security checks.

This continued for several weeks until one evening he failed to rendezvous with a working party to return to the camp as arranged and we were all very worried. We were all hoping that he was safe and that he had succeeded in getting on a ship and was even now on his way across the Baltic on the first stage of his journey home.

Unfortunately our hopes were not realised and a few days afterwards we were told that we would have to provide a guard of honour and pall-bearers for a funeral. We discovered that the funeral was for our friend from the RAF but it was some time before we heard the full story of his death and apparently he had been going up the gangway of a Swedish ship when a German patrol called on him to halt; he made a run for it but he had no chance and they shot and killed him.

Everybody in the camp was saddened and thoroughly depressed when the full story emerged and some prisoners, although by now hardened characters, broke down and wept; undoubtedly it was a very sad end to a long and dangerous attempt to escape by a very brave man.

We had a party of Swiss representatives from the International Red Cross visit the camp to confirm that we were being treated in accordance with the Geneva Convention and although, as a matter of principle, we made many complaints about the lack of German food and shortage of items to purchase with our Lagergeldt wages, we didn't get any encouragement and certainly nothing changed.

Shortly after this visit we heard that seriously wounded or very ill prisoners were going to be sent to Sweden as a first stage on the journey home. This news naturally inspired every prisoner to devise some means of being included and quite a few prisoners suddenly developed mysterious illnesses or feigned mental illness.

Some were attempting to show symptoms of every illness known to man and, I suspect, there were even some that had never been diagnosed before. There were many genuine cases of tuberculosis, after-effects of frostbite and some unfortunates who really were suffering mentally, but I personally never saw or heard of any prisoners successfully getting away with faking it and I do not think any were taken who were not genuinely ill.

Unsuccessful attempts included a chap who tried every way he could think of to encourage a guard to shoot him, preferably in a leg or arm, and there was another chap who actually chopped a finger off but even then he was unsuccessful.

I suddenly developed severe stomach pains but the German doctor who examined me couldn't have been very well-qualified because he ignored my cries of agony and really was quite unsympathetic and he had the gall to tell me I was lucky enough to get sufficient food to give me indigestion and both the pain and the symptoms would disappear if only I worked harder.

If my memory serves me correctly the only chaps from our camp to be given a passage home were three who were genuinely suffering, one from tuberculosis, one very sad mental case and Johnny Nicholls because of the severe wounds he had received while wiping out a German machine gun post to earn his VC. These prisoners were taken by ambulance to join the 'Trotting Home' which was the prisoners nickname for the Swedish ship the SS Drottingholm that would be taking the prisoners across the Baltic to Sweden but in view of their condition none of us who were left behind really envied them.

Towards the end of September 1943 we heard about the Allied invasion of Sicily and this cheered us up but many were still saying we had to have an invasion of Northern Europe i.e. France or the Low Countries and there was continuing bad news from the Far East where the Japanese seemed unbeatable.

We started to plan for another Christmas in captivity and the rehearsals began for a pantomime which had been written by some of the prisoners and included songs and sketches based on our lives as soldiers and prisoners.

One example of a short song written for this production was:

Roll out the Army,
The Navy as well.
Roll out the Air Force,
The Marines are looking swell.
We have the big guns,
The Bombers as well,
So now's the time to roll together
And knock old Hitler and his gang to Hell.

(This song nearly resulted in an early finale because rather surprisingly, some of the Germans didn't like it.) There was another much longer song with lyrics by Sid Bonner (sung to the tune of 'Bye Bye Blackbird'), as follows:

Bye Bye Danzig,
Pick up all the kit I've got,
Leave behind my wooden cot.
Bye Bye Danzig,
Make my own way down to the sea,
Where a troopship waits for me.
Bye Bye Danzig,
No more early roll calls in the morning,
We'll hear no more bloody Germans bawling.
Danzig City may be fine,
Give me that old town of mine,
Danzig Bye Bye.
Though we've been here for three long years,
We'll put an end to all your fears.
Soon we're leaving,
To see old Blighty's shores again,

And hop on board the next boat-train.
No more grieving,
Wives, sweethearts, mothers.
We'll be meeting,
Tears of joy and loving words of greeting,
So grin and bear it all you chaps,
We'll be home this year and no perhaps,
Danzig Bye Bye.

We really could not understand why the Germans didn't like the songs. Could it have been our singing?

But to get back to the main story. The weather was so bad that work on the building site was stopped for the winter as usual and we were again allocated to different working parties to go on various jobs around the town. Together with about twenty others I had to march to the other side of Danzig past the docks to an old iron foundry and warehouse. Our job mainly consisted of pushing barrows which we had slowly and painstakingly loaded with various items of ironmongery and then transferring the items to lorries, both army and civilian, presumably for distribution all over the area. Surprisingly none of the drivers ever came over to thank us for the exceedingly long rest periods they were getting as a result of our very thorough and slow loading and unloading, so I am not sure whether they were grateful or not.

The whole camp was soon supplied with new saucepans of various sizes, frying pans, hobnails for boots and a very large supply of screws and nails to be used for any improvisations the prisoners wanted to make to their living accommodation or to the facilities in the concert hall.

On the way back to the camp every night the main road we were walking along became mysteriously covered with all sorts of tacks and nails and we were praying for a large increase in punctures, hopefully for military vehicles. I and the rest of the prisoners in my room managed to scrounge a large milk churn and some copper tubing and in no time at all we had fixed up our own small distillery which was well hidden in the air raid shelter in front of our hut. Everything imaginable was thrown into the churn but mainly potato peelings.

A couple of chaps from our room were on a working party which was carrying out general cleaning and washing down of painted walls in a large building next to a hospital which was mainly occupied by a medical institute and a laboratory. One of the items that was scrounged from this establishment proved to be a large bottle of pure alcohol which one idiot sampled neat with the result that not only was his mouth badly burnt, but the shock caused him to collapse unconscious on the floor. Whether this was the result of the alcohol or the sudden pain of the burns I don't know but he got little sympathy from any of us. Anyhow, fortunately he recovered fully in a few days but I noticed that he refused a second drink from the bottle.

We decided that the contents of the bottle would make a marvellous addition to the contents of the distillery and would add some body and possibly a nice bouquet. Judging by the rapid bubbling and gurgling as soon as we added it, I'm sure it must have achieved something.

Christmas came and the amateur chefs in the various groups excelled themselves with some of the meals that were conjured up from the contents of the Red Cross parcels and the extra items obtained by bartering, or in a few cases, stolen from the Germans.

The pantomime was again a huge success, particularly the principal boy which traditionally was supposed to be a girl, and the chorus 'girls' who were expertly made up.

I must say that even after sampling a good amount of the fiendish brew from our distillery together with some schnapps, my imagination still wouldn't stretch to having lustful thoughts about either the principal boy or any of the chorus girls.

Most of the prisoners, especially those in our room, were in various stages of drunkenness and were either singing songs (mostly rude), fighting among themselves or had already collapsed unconscious on to the floor or had managed to stagger to their bunk and collapse. The general opinion seemed to be that, under the circumstances, a good time was had by all. But in the morning the majority of us had thick heads and anyone who had made the slightest noise would have risked being murdered.

Rather surprisingly quite a few subscribed to the old saying, 'The hair of the dog is a good cure' and they started to check that the distillery was completely empty and then turned their attention to any bottles they could find laying around and drained the dregs from them.

A few of the chaps felt so ill that they reported sick but they got little sympathy from the Medical Officer who told them that the best cure for their condition was to run round the camp perimeter twenty times and then do another hour's exercise.

Chapter 14

Happy New Year!

New Year's Day 1944 dawned, and as expected most of us had thick heads again from the previous evening's drinking session. Like most of the prisoners I was making New Year's resolutions which included the following or similar thoughts: renew efforts to find a way home; steal or scrounge as much food or other articles from the Germans as possible; do as little work as possible; and cause the Germans as many problems as humanly possible.

We fell in as usual for early morning roll-call and as usual the Germans were still having problems with their counting and despite encouraging comments from the prisoners they couldn't agree the number of prisoners on parade with their lists.

Obviously the prisoners were highly delighted and in addition to sarcastic comments they began offering their fingers to help in the counting. Of course several were only offering two upright fingers. Some of the guards were dispatched to make an urgent search of the camp and then we heard a voice singing 'Scottish Songs'. Round the corner of the hut on to the parade ground staggered a figure dressed in a kilt, clasping an empty bottle.

It was Jock Humphries from our room. Although he was in the Black Watch he was really a Yorkshireman from Castleford, but in some respects he appeared more Scottish than a true-born Highlander.

The prisoners all began clapping and cheering and joined Jock in the singing, but having no sense of humour the Germans didn't think it was very funny and he was escorted off the parade ground and he had to spend the next two weeks in the cooler and when he returned to the camp he said, 'I needed that time to sober up and it was a good change from a working party anyway'.

A couple of nights later we had another even more remarkable occurrence when all the occupants in my room were suddenly wakened by a loud voice shouting. It turned out to be Ernie Rowbotham, a Manchester bus driver before the war, who was recounting his experiences in France during the fighting in 1940.

We all listened spellbound as he was reliving his past and it was the usual story of how they were outnumbered and outgunned until finally they were surrounded and had no alternative but to surrender. Ernie was describing his feelings of despair and then said he was in a ditch and saw this German officer standing above him pointing a gun at him, so he raised his arms above his head and then gave a terrible scream. If there had still been anyone asleep in the room they would have certainly been wakened by that awful noise and it was at that moment that Ernie woke up.

When he had recovered and was fully awake we told him what had been happening, and he told us how the officer had shot him and that reliving that awful moment had caused him to scream and wake up. The shot had knocked him out and the officer had apparently left him for dead, but in fact the bullet had embedded itself in a cheap pocket-watch in his breast pocket which had saved his life.

He still had the pocket-watch which he had managed to keep hidden and after rummaging through his belongings he produced it to show us; unbelievably it still had the bullet in it.

Life returned to what passed as normal in the camp but the story of Ernie's dream spread and was the main topic of conversation for several days. We returned to the usual practice of working on various jobs around the area and as usual one of the wintertime jobs required some working parties to go out on the annual ice and snow-clearing exercise. Fortunately I managed to stay on the working party going to the iron foundry and we were praying that there would not be any stocktaking while we were still working there. Nevertheless this fear did not deter us from again taking saucepans, frying pans, nails and screws with which we were even able to barter with the Poles working on Stolzenberg for large farmhouse loaves. We also continued with our nightly distribution of hazards for the unsuspecting motorists i.e. nails and screws sprinkled across the road.

The weather improved slightly and we were taken off the iron foundry detail and some of us were put on a new working party which involved groups of four of us travelling on an open-top lorry with a guard to and from a brickyard about thirty miles from Stolzenberg. Our job was to build up stocks of bricks on the building site. Apparently they had completely run out of bricks on the site and this was an emergency exercise to build up enough stocks to last all through the summer.

The ride was quite pleasant as the weather was now quite spring-like and it made a lovely change to get away from the area of the camp and the building site. We discovered there were Polish girls working in the brickyard and from then on we always tried to time it so that our lorry was in the brickyard at the time when we could spend our lunch break there. It made a pleasant diversion for us to take it in turns to try and persuade the girls to come round behind the stacks of bricks while the rest of the party diverted the attention of the guards.

Handling the bricks was very hard on the hands so we scrounged pieces of rubber inner tube and cut them to cover our palms and fingers with slots cut to fit over our fingers and thumbs. This gave a lot of protection to our hands and we used to load the lorry with one chap on the ground throwing four bricks together to a chap catching them on the lorry and stacking them until the lorry was full.

The prisoners and guard would then climb up on to the top of the bricks for the return journey to the building site at Stolzenberg where we would reverse the procedure and unload and build the bricks into large stacks. Unfortunately after a few weeks despite all our efforts to slow down the work, there were sufficient bricks on the site and the lorry journeys stopped and we had to return to our normal jobs on the estate.

In an effort to get more production from the prisoners, the Germans offered a system of daily quotas i.e. bricklayers were to lay a specified number of bricks and then they would be allowed to pack up work for the day. We mistrusted the Germans and in any case we did not want to appear too eager, so we refused point blank.

Then began a period of arguments, threats and discussion until we finally agreed for a trial period to accept quotas which meant that if we worked at a reasonable speed we could finish in about four hours and still only lay about twenty more bricks than we had been doing. The fact that we were in a position to get the Germans even to discuss such a thing, let alone agree to our figures, illustrates the amazing difference between our relations with the Germans now and in 1940.

By now we had a fairly good idea of how the German mind worked so we agreed amongst ourselves that we would make the quotas last all day and in fact on a couple of occasions we even finished a few minutes later than previously. However after a few weeks we gradually began to finish a little earlier, and just to help things along we 'assisted' the German foreman to count the bricks so that on many occasions we were actually laying as much as one hundred bricks less than before the quota system had started. As our rate of work increased so the standards got worse, but the civilian foremen overlooked this aspect because they were under strict instructions that they must achieve their targets of building completion which made it impossible for them to make us take down any bricks and re-lay them.

The weather now was much better and with beautiful sunny days we were able to work stripped to the waist which meant that although we all had lovely sun tans, we still longed to be on a sunny beach back home or maybe having a picnic on the banks of the Thames at Windsor even without the sun tan.

We kept hearing of advances on the Italian Front and of the landings at Anzio but still no good news seemed to be coming from the Far East. Our nights were occasionally disturbed by air raid warnings when Russian bombers flew over our camp but they were always so high that the searchlights rarely found them and most of the anti-aircraft guns never bothered to open fire. The news from the Russian Front was still not good for the Germans, although according to their newspapers they were still holding their own and any troop movements on the front were because they were taking up more strategic positions.

There were continuous rumours of a second front in France with the result that, coupled with the situation on the Eastern Front, German morale was getting low and their attitude to the prisoners was becoming more and more apologetic. In fact, with one or two exceptions, they tried to give the impression that they had always really been friends of the British. It was now almost impossible to find a German who had been a Nazi or who had even supported Hitler although they were always very careful that no other German could overhear them voicing those opinions or suggesting they were against the war or Hitler.

The camp Commandant and a few of his officers were outwardly, at least, the exception and were still carrying on as if they were winning the war. They issued an order that all tins in the Red Cross parcels must be punctured before issue to prevent any prisoner from building up a stock of foodstuffs to take with him on any escape attempt.

This practice was very annoying but we managed to put a brave face on it and taunted the Germans saying they were only puncturing the tins to smell what real food smells like instead of the watery kartoffel (potato) soup they had to exist on. We were still very glad when the Germans suddenly seemed to get fed up with the practice and we again began to get the parcels unopened.

We had some excitement at Easter when the air raid sirens sounded at about lunch time and we saw wave after wave of Flying Fortresses circling over the camp and we all stood there waving and cheering. It appeared that the camp had been a rendezvous point from where all the aircraft flew off towards Gotenhafen (Gydnia).

The air was filled with strips of tinfoil dropped by the aircraft which we understood later were intended to confuse the German radar and guns. We also heard later that the planes had bombed a fighter-plane factory which had only just been rebuilt. (The bombing actually started five minutes before the official opening ceremony.) Although we heard that there had been many casualties including some very high ranking Luftwaffe officers we were unable to get any confirmation of the story.

Once again we returned to the same old boring routine until one day one of the working parties brought back a chap who said he was a Czech who had joined the Allies in

London where he had enlisted in the Air Force and subsequently while on a bombing mission had been taken prisoner. But after spending some time in a Luftstalag he had managed to escape.

His story and his general manner was very plausible, but for some unexplainable reason several of the prisoners including me were very suspicious. After questioning him about London and the Air Force, some of his answers made us conclude that it could be very risky to allow him to stay as we suspected he may be a German plant. As it would be inadvisable to let him discover too many of the camp secrets he was kept under very secure guard. Some of the lads were in favour of killing him there and then, but since we had not been able to prove whether he was a plant or not we did not agree. He had not been allowed to learn anything of importance so it was decided by a majority vote that he should be escorted out of the camp and accordingly the next morning the same working party that had brought him in took him out and told him to try another camp, make an effort on his own or make his way back to his Luftstalag.

The rumours about a second front were becoming more frequent and one enterprising individual began running a book on the date and place for the invasion. The most popular place was Calais but the dates varied from May to August.

The prison life was affecting many of the prisoners in odd ways and some withdrew into themselves and became virtual recluses whilst others became more extrovert as for example one chap who always dressed up in a complete cowboy outfit which he had managed to get sent out by his family. I imagine they thought he wanted it for a show but it was really amusing when you saw him walking round the camp wearing a large stetson hat and all his other cowboy clothes. But the Germans, with some justification, thought he was completely mad and refused to let him have even wooden guns so he could pretend to draw and shoot. There was another chap who we really felt sorry for because he had been seriously affected mentally and he used to walk round the perimeter of the camp for hours on end twirling a piece of coal on the end of a length of string.

One morning the Germans announced that they were going to cut the bread ration, and although this would not make any significant difference to us because we were really living on the contents of the Red Cross parcels, it still made us mad. More for a laugh than any other reason we made banners which read, 'Keine Brot – Keine Arbeit' (No Bread – No Work) and paraded up and down just inside the wire by the main gate and directly opposite the German quarters. At the same time we were shouting out the same slogan at the top of our voices.

A few minutes after the start of our protest the Germans came out of their huts and they and the guards on duty at the gate shouted at us to return to our huts but they were only greeted with rude signs and comments about their ancestry.

This demonstration continued for another half an hour and then the guards marched in to the camp and ordered us to fall in for roll-call and after threatening gestures with their guns we slowly began to fall in on the parade ground. While this had been taking place several of the guards had been going round all the huts and rousing all the other prisoners telling them to join us on the parade ground. The Germans started their usual attempts at counting amid sarcastic shouts ridiculing their efforts to get the numbers right and rude comments about the cut bread ration.

To our great surprise we saw a tank and several lorries arrive at the main gate. The lorries came in to draw up in a line facing us whilst the tank was positioned at the main gate with its gun pointing at us. Out of the lorries came a number of Germans armed with machine guns who took up strategic positions all round us. There were also about thirty civilians who we recognised as Gestapo by their manner and dress. The Gestapo went into the concert hall and the guards started taking prisoners in after them On arrival the prisoners were ordered to strip in front of two Gestapo men and while one searched the clothing the other searched the prisoner, when it came to my turn he looked into my mouth and then to my horror he even looked into my back passage. After the search the prisoners were taken back to their positions on the parade ground. At the same time there were parties of Gestapo men searching all the huts. Unfortunately this resulted in their confiscating about three lorry-loads full of contraband including a camera, radio, several farmhouse loaves, eggs, a few sheath knives, electrical equipment and a large amount of wood and coal which we used in the stove for heating and cooking. However, there were many items which fortunately they did not discover.

When we were eventually allowed back to our huts we discovered it was in a terrible mess with uprooted floor-boards and strips of moulding taken down from the walls. Nobby Clark said, 'All this fuss over a tiny piece of bread and a small demonstration – what on earth will they do when we start cheering and shouting because of the Second Front?'

It was shortly after this episode when we did in fact hear about the D-Day landings and it turned out that one chap had correctly forecast the actual day thus scooping the jackpot of Lagergeldt although nobody had succeeded in forecasting the correct landing places. Naturally all the prisoners were very excited and wasted no time in telling the German guards that their days were numbered, and did they wish to surrender to us immediately so that we could give them preferential treatment and possibly protect them from the Russians? Strangely enough none of them would go that far although it was blatantly obvious that they were considerably shaken by the news.

Rather foolishly we thought that in a few weeks it would be all over and we would be on our way home. We also heard that the Russians were advancing from the east and you could see the Germans were getting very frightened mainly because of the tales of the way that the Russians were supposed to be taking their revenge on any Germans they captured, civilians as well as soldiers.

Since our camp was much nearer to the Russians than the Allies in the west all the Germans in Danzig were very frightened indeed. Also at about this time stories were circulating about attempts on Hitler's life and the general opinion was that the officers involved deserved to die not for attempting to kill him, but because they had failed.

We also heard about the heavy fighting in Normandy and of course Londoners in particular were very worried about the stories of Flying Bombs raining down on London.

Although work was still continuing after a fashion on the building site, the prisoners were only really concerned about getting the latest news of the fighting and in August we heard that the Allies were making some advances in France.

We also heard about the Warsaw uprising and were all thoroughly disgusted when we heard how the Russians had stood by and failed to go to the assistance of the Poles in their brave fight against the Germans. The news of the fighting in the Far East was also slowly improving but we were saddened when we heard about the fighting at Arnhem. This tragic news, together with the news of the collapse of the Warsaw uprising again aroused feelings of indignation amongst the prisoners who were all disgusted by the apparently stupid errors at Arnhem which cost the

Parachute Regiment so many casualties and the apparent cold-hearted indifference of the Russians to the fate of the partisans fighting in Warsaw.

News of the German counter attacks in the west particularly around Bastogne caused a lot of dismay and anxiety amongst the prisoners and I certainly recalled that Bastogne was the first place where we had climbed into cattle trucks during our Cook's Tour through France, Belgium etc. when we had been taken prisoner in 1940.

At last we began to hear really good news about the Far East although in our position we considered the news in Europe to be the most important although I personally was very worried about my eldest brother Ted who I knew was in the Far East somewhere as a bombardier in the Royal Artillery.

Christmas arrived again and although shows were put on with the usual expertise and everybody was trying to put a brave face on things, nevertheless there were strong feelings of gloom and despondency – mainly because when the invasion took place in June we never dreamt that we would be spending another Christmas in this camp and morale was rock-bottom. Most of the prisoners had made the usual efforts and had succeeded in getting a good supply of drinks and of course were quite naturally attempting to drown their sorrows by drinking themselves into oblivion which certainly helped in the short term but the effects soon wore off and fits of depression returned.

Soon after Christmas we heard that the German counter-attack had finally been repelled and they were being forced to retreat on all fronts. We were still very worried by the persistent stories of Flying Bombs falling on London and we kept hoping that the Allied advance would speed up to overrun the place where they were being launched from thus bringing to an end the terrible bombardments.

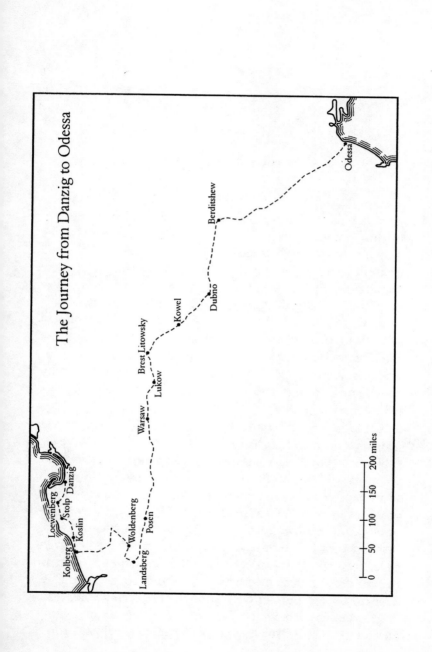

The Journey from Danzig to Odessa

Chapter 15

Leaving Stolzenberg

The dawning of 18th February, 1945 marked an important turning point in our lives as prisoners because that was the day that we were issued with Red Cross parcels and cigarettes and told to pack as many of our belongings as we could carry on a march that was intended to take us away from the Russian advance and further into Germany.

At eleven o'clock in the morning we paraded for roll-call and after the numbers were agreed we marched out of the gates of Stolzenberg Camp for the last time. The weather was absolutely appalling with the ground covered with snow and ice and the temperature was several degrees below freezing.

I find it very difficult to describe my feelings when I was leaving the camp that had been my home for a few years. Obviously I was very pleased to be starting on a journey which would hopefully lead towards home but I was still apprehensive about marching into Germany and wondered what awaited us at the end of the journey. As we approached the main road leading out of Danzig we were brought to a halt whilst an astonishing and horrific cavalcade consisting of men, hardly recognisable as human beings, dressed in striped hats, jackets and trousers went by. The men were pulling on ropes which were attached to a large wooden sled which I estimated to be about twenty feet long, eight feet wide and six feet high which was three quarters full of figures in striped outfits who had been piled on top of each other. Even as we watched one of the prisoners who had been pulling on a rope just collapsed on to the road and in complete silence others picked him up and tossed him like a bag of straw on to the pile of bodies in the sled.

Although there had been several of them who had lifted him up you could see that they had an awful job throwing the body up on to the sled mainly because they were in such a starved and emaciated condition; in fact they just resembled bags of bones. It dawned on us that these poor unfortunate human beings must be from one of the many concentration camps we had heard about but none of the stories could have prepared us for the unbelievably dreadful sight before our eyes and the smell and appearance of these poor wretches was so bad I was physically sick.

The realisation of what these prisoners must have suffered and were still going through made our imprisonment seem like a picnic in comparison and the sight certainly increased my hatred for the Germans.

Shortly after this we were joined by other Allied prisoners from various camps and eventually there was a column of about one thousand five hundred prisoners. After marching for about twenty kilometres, five of us – Bob, Doug, Paddy, Bill and myself – decided that going further into Germany, with an unknown destination and outcome was too risky so we watched for a suitable moment and managed to get away from the column without being detected.

That night we spent in a barn but were rudely awakened by German guards who kicked and used their rifle butts on us, forcing us to march quickly until we caught up with the column which had spent the night in a nearby village hall. Our return was sarcastically greeted by the other prisoners who made remarks like 'Trust you lot to be late as usual' and 'We knew you wouldn't be able to leave us'.

We marched through a town called Karthaus and then approached a small village called Gartsch where we again performed our disappearing act, but this time we found a friendly Polish family who took us into their home and fed us. I will always remember sitting down with them to listen to a speech by Winston Churchill on their radio after which we slept in a workshop attached to the house.

The next morning we sat down to a large breakfast of eggs and bacon which I was thoroughly enjoying when suddenly the door opposite to where I was sitting burst open and it was filled by a snarling German shepherd dog and an SS trooper. My first thought when I recovered from the shock was that I must finish my breakfast and I started shovelling the rest of the food into my mouth as fast as I possibly could.

Amidst a lot of shouting and barking we got the distinct impression that they wanted us outside and as we went through the door we were confronted by more SS troopers with dogs. We were helped on our way with kicks and smacks from rifle butts and marched off to eventually arrive at a village square in Schmellen.

We were greeted by two SS officers who instructed the troopers to take us in to a room behind a cafe and give us a few good, hard hits with their rifles which was supposed to teach us not to escape again. We understood enough German so we were expecting the blows and we were able to protect our faces and heads to some extent but we still got a very painful beating until finally they kicked us into a small windowless room with an armed SS trooper and a dog standing guard outside.

Despite our own predicament we were more worried about the consequences to the Polish family for their assistance to us. Although we tried to tell the SS officers that the family had not known that we were prisoners and that we had only just arrived at the house a few minutes before their own arrival, they ignored what we were saying and told us to keep quiet.

After several hours the SS Troopers ordered us outside and marched us back to Karthaus. In the main square stood a large building which turned out to be the Law Courts for the area and we were marched into the building and up to the first floor along a corridor, which was lined by frightened civilians, until being told to stop and wait outside some large double doors. After a short wait the door opened and I was pushed inside into what turned out to be a very large room with no furniture except for a huge desk at the opposite end of the room, towards which I was pushed by a German soldier. Behind the large desk sat a well-built individual in a Brown Shirt uniform with a black swastika armband. On the wall behind him was a large picture of Adolf Hitler and in a chair by the side of the desk sat another evil-looking man who told me that he was a Gestapo officer and that I was to be shot as a spy. They then proceeded to take turns to ask me questions to which I kept replying, 'I am an English soldier. My name is J. Roberts and my Army number is 6896551'. This was followed by a lot of hysterical shouting by both the Brown Shirt and the Gestapo officers which coincided with frequent hits by rifles wielded by two SS troopers who had been called into the room by the Gestapo officer.

I got fed up with picking myself up off the floor and much to my relief they decided to give up on me and I was taken out of the room, feeling very sore and not knowing whether or not I was going to be shot. My appearance must have shaken my pals but I said in passing, 'Ignore the Gestapo and Brown Shirt bastards. Only give name and number', for which I got another whack and was shouted at and made to wait further down the corridor.

After all the prisoners had suffered a similar process we were marched out of the town to a farm and told to climb up into a hay loft where we promptly went to sleep while guards remained outside all night. Next morning we were escorted to a large camp called Socressen and pushed into a hut.

Later when things seemed to have quietened down a bit I decided to investigate and found that the SS troopers had been replaced by Wehrmacht guards who were not as efficient or watchful.

I was lucky enough to find a hole in the fence through which I squeezed and went wandering through some woods until I came out the other side and found myself on a small farm. Going into a barn I met a Polish girl who told me the farm belonged to her parents and that her name was Halina. I told her my name and explained who I was and she gave me some bread and cheese which I washed down with some lovely fresh milk after which I felt so exhausted that I just collapsed on some hay and immediately fell asleep.

When I awoke it was dark and shortly afterwards Halina returned carrying an oil lamp and some food. We spent a long time talking and she explained that her parents were too scared to let me go into the farmhouse in case the Germans found me there. Recalling my recent capture in a Polish house I could understand their fears and I had no wish to be responsible for getting any more people into trouble. As it was now getting quite late, Halina said she had better go back to the farmhouse to stop her parents from getting worried.

The next morning Halina brought me an egg-and-bacon breakfast with fresh milk and afterwards I helped her to clean out the animals. We spent the rest of the day butter-making in a large wooden contraption that revolved round an axle. It was very hard work and took me ages to get the hang of turning the weird contraption, but Halina seemed to manage it without any problems so I suppose it all came down to practice and acquired expertise.

That evening I decided to go back to the camp to find out what was happening and stupidly got caught by guards who hit me with their rifles and threw me into the hut with the rest of the gang, I told them of my exploits which made them very jealous, especially when I went into some details about the food. They said I must want my head examining to have come back to the camp and by this time I was inclined to agree with them. I definitely regretted my decision to return more and more with each passing minute, and I couldn't explain why I had decided to come back and I deeply regretted not having the opportunity to say a proper goodbye to Halina.

Next morning nine of us – Bob, Doug, Paddy, Les, Larry, Bill, Ed, Min, and myself – were marched to the railway station under armed guard and pushed aboard the train into a passenger carriage which was an unusual method of travel for us. Within a few minutes the train started off and we arrived at a place called Loewenburg at about one o'clock and were kept hanging around until midnight and then pushed on to our usual mode of transport i.e. a cattle truck. The train left and finally arrived at a place called Stolp and it was now five o'clock in the morning. We jumped out of the cattle truck and were immediately marched out of the station and up a long hill to the Belling Kaserne which was a cavalry barracks.

Shortly after our arrival we were told to start cleaning the barracks after which they promised we would get food, so we did the cleaning as quickly as we could. If our old RSM at Tidworth Barracks had inspected them he would have had a heart attack or at least high blood pressure, but fortunately nobody came to inspect the rooms and we were given a bowl of watery soup with a small slice of black bread.

Guards took us to a loft above the cavalry stables where we lay down and fell asleep on the hay. The next day was spent talking and discussing ideas and various plans until a guard took us to get some of the usual watery soup and black bread and marched us back to the loft where we continued our discussions and decided we had travelled about 175 kms from Danzig.

The following morning was 26th February and we were marched from the barracks to the railway station where we climbed into our usual cattle truck for a journey which finished at a place called Freytz where we were put into a barn for the night. During the night three prisoners decided they wanted to go for a walk and succeeded in getting out through a very small hole they had made in the wall of the barn. At ten o'clock the next morning when the guards discovered there were three missing there was a hell of a row but we were taken back to the railway station to continue our journey until we arrived at a place called Kalwitz where we spent another night in a barn and had the usual soup and bread. The following day our journey took us to Zanow where our resting place was a gymnasium. The floor was very hard and uncomfortable and I didn't see anyone rushing to do exercises.

Our next stop was at Koslin where our temporary home was a large wooden hut. In the far distance we could see German Stuka Bombers diving and apparently trying to halt the advance of Russian tanks which until that moment we had no idea were anywhere near us.

After a very noisy night with the constant drone of aircraft we heard the sound of frenzied activity next door which turned out to be a food store. All the contents were being distributed to civilians so we got out by forcing a space in the back wall and managed to convince the

German in charge of the distribution that we were refugees from East Prussia. I suppose that strictly speaking that was true and anyhow, we got some bread, meat and cigarettes while the soldiers detailed to guard us were too busy grabbing everything they could for themselves to notice or be bothered about us also getting supplies.

It was very obvious that the soldiers and civilians were very scared of the Russians and soon the guards got us moving again as they did not want to wait to meet the Russians and wanted to get as far into Germany as they could.

We arrived at a town called Kolberg and were put into another barn for the night. By this time we were sick of the continual hustling along and in any case we again thought there would be no advantage for us to be in central Germany, so we came to the conclusion that our journey west had gone on for about 300 kms and was long enough so we made up our minds that at the first opportunity we would get away from the guards and try to get through the Russian lines. We succeeded in making a hole in the back wall of the barn after some considerable effort and scrambled through without arousing the guards. It was really a spur of the moment decision in the end which we were lucky to get away with and in a way our decision was a bit surprising when you consider all the stories we had heard about the Russians. We had no way of knowing what sort of reception we would get, always supposing we were successful in reaching their lines, and of course there was the added problem that none of us could speak Russian.

Chapter 16

Meeting the Russians

We left the town keeping under cover of hedgerows and trees and made our way carefully and slowly towards the area where we had seen the Stukas, and before long we heard the sound of heavy gunfire and then to our utter amazement we saw coming down the road towards us a column of Russian tanks. We thought we were dreaming when we saw on the top of the second tank a Russian soldier sitting down playing a piano accordion. We all started cheering and waving to them while shouting 'Tovarich' and 'Angelski' (English) and some of the Russians waved back to us.

After about thirty tanks had rumbled by we were treated to another incredible sight as we saw strolling along the pavement towards us as if she was out for a Sunday afternoon stroll in Moscow, a very attractive woman in Russian uniform with Red Cross badges on her arms and we assumed she was either a doctor or a nurse. Of course one chap had to say, 'Can you imagine her taking your temperature and tucking you up in bed?' and we all said at the same time that we could dream. We tried to speak to her but as none of us could speak Russian it was a bit difficult. We indicated friendship and pointing in the direction we were going, we said, 'Moscow' which made her laugh and nod in agreement.

Continuing along this main road we could hear heavy gunfire on both sides which was getting closer so we assumed we must be getting near to the Russian front lines. Then suddenly we heard the awful scream of Stukas and we threw ourselves into the ditch. The sight of the Stukas dive-bombing brought back unhappy memories of the fighting in Calais and the hideous screaming when they bombed the railway station while we were inside having a meal, but we cheered up a lot when the gunfire increased and we saw two Stukas falling to the ground in flames. Shortly after this we were going past a large house and, hearing gunfire quite close, we dived to the ground. There were loud explosions and at least two direct hits on the house. The front of it was practically demolished.

We beat a hasty retreat and after about five miles we entered and explored an empty house, decided it was safe and made ourselves comfortable for the night.

The next morning we continued along the main road and came to the conclusion that this was a narrow spearhead advance by the Russians because there was still continuous heavy gunfire on both sides of the road. As we travelled through a village called Shiverlergin the sound of battle increased in volume all round us so we decided that as it was now late afternoon, we had better start looking for a place to spend the night. We saw a farm some distance back from the road which looked as if it would be worth investigating.

When we got to the farm it appeared to be deserted and fairly safe so we decided to spend the night there. Unfortunately the heavy gunfire continued all through the night so we didn't get much sleep and at times it seemed as if we were in the centre of the fighting, but to leave the farm in the middle of the night was out of the question because there was always the danger of the Russians firing at us by mistake or of us walking into German positions.

Early the next morning we still couldn't fathom out what was happening so we followed some civilians down a narrow road. Suddenly there was pandemonium as we came under fire and Bill, Ed, Min, Bob and myself dived into some bushes and began crawling back in the direction we had just come from. For about one hundred yards we were under constant machine gun fire but miraculously none of us got hit, but unfortunately during this incident, Doug Paddy, Les and Larry, who had caught up with us got themselves captured by SS troopers.

The rest of us got back to the main road and started going eastwards. Shortly we were going past several Russian machine gun posts and it became obvious to us that these were the guns that had fired at us. Bob said, 'With friends like that, who needs enemies?'

We continued along this road for the rest of the day until eventually we came to a small village and decided to spend the night in one of the deserted houses. There was plenty of choice because it was obvious that all of the German inhabitants had been really frightened of being captured by the Russians and had all fled towards Germany.

The next morning we had a pleasant surprise when the four who had been captured by the SS rejoined us and told us that the SS had made them carry stretchers with badly wounded troopers on them. There had been about twenty SS with the majority of them suffering from wounds of various descriptions.

When they had stopped for the night in a forest, our four pals had escaped and by a strange coincidence had reached the crossroads at the same time as we had from an entirely different direction, and so much to our great relief we had been re-united.

At the next town we went into a very large house to find it was occupied by Russian officers who invited us to stay and gave us a lovely pork supper which was the best meal we had eaten for a long time. The large reception room on the ground floor had a beautiful grand piano in one corner and later in the evening we heard it being played while all the Russians were gathered round singing. We went downstairs from the luxurious bedrooms we had been told we could use and much to our surprise found that as well as the officers who we had seen on our arrival, there were now several Russian women in uniform who I believe were all doctors and nurses. All the Russians gave us the distinct impression that the main objective of the evening was to get drunk as quickly as possible.

They all looked as if they were enjoying themselves and didn't have a care in the world. Then the pianist was joined by an accordionist and a fiddler and some of the Russians must have still been fairly sober because they were performing Russian dances with lots of knee-bending, arm-waving and shouting.

We all thought it was marvellous entertainment but it was nearly ruined for me when a Russian soldier staggered in through the front door waving a gun and whether he thought I was an enemy or not I do not know but he certainly appeared to be threatening to shoot me. It was fortunate for me that one of the Russian officers stepped in front of me and started shouting at the soldier and then slapped him round the face several times and pushed him back out of the door, after which the evening continued and we all thoroughly enjoyed ourselves.

We all had terrible hangovers the next morning which was the main reason for us not wishing to leave the house; none of us felt like moving at all never mind walking any distance. That night we had a similar evening except that we managed to refrain from drinking so much and we were glad we did when we discovered that some of the Russians were filling bottles from drums of kerosene and drinking it.

In view of what they were drinking it was not surprising that as the evening wore on, the Russians began arguing among themselves but when they started firing their guns we decided that discretion was the better part of valour and we beat a hasty retreat upstairs to our bedrooms and barricaded ourselves in.

After a reasonable night's sleep we decided, in view of the previous night's fighting and gunplay, that it might be wiser to continue our journey. So we started walking eastwards and went through places called Gross and Klein Silber, Alt Labitz, Friedland and Reetz. Unfortunately somewhere along the way Larry and Doug must have wandered off because we lost them but another ex-prisoner called Paul joined us.

It was now 13th March and having travelled about 400 kms from Danzig everyone was fed up with walking and it became a priority to find some means of transport. We were lucky enough to find a horse and an old hay cart in a barn so we commandeered them and after harnessing the horse we all clambered aboard the hay cart and away we went. Although it was very slow progress, it was much better than walking.

We got a very pleasant surprise at the next farm we came to because in the barn we found a very elegant old-fashioned coach with highly polished bodywork and glass windows. High up in front was a seat for the driver and his assistant and in fact it was very similar to carriages used in the Royal or Lord Mayoral processions in England.

Unfortunately there were no horses on the farm but in a field behind the barn we found a mule, which after a lot of effort we managed to catch and by means of a modified harness fixed it so that he would be able to pull the coach on his own.

The following day at another farm we were lucky enough to find a pony and trap so our transport was rapidly increasing. We concentrated on searching all the abandoned houses very thoroughly and taking anything which we thought might be worth acquiring and then loaded the items on to the hay wagon. Some of the finds were unusual, e.g. a top hat, a bugle and an old-fashioned coat with tails.

We seldom saw any civilians which was perhaps just as well because our column must have been a very strange sight led by a mule-drawn coach with a small Cockney driver resplendent in top hat and tails sitting high up in front and next to him was a scruffy looking individual who was continually blowing 'Do you ken John Peel' and various Army calls on a bugle.

The coach was followed by me driving the pony and trap with the old hay cart bringing up the rear, piled high with every conceivable type of object that we had collected.

I suppose that we looked on it as a form of reparation – the rest of the gang, with some weird-looking individuals among them, were distributed among the three vehicles.

The next afternoon we were being passed by a large Polish convoy going in the direction we had just come from when suddenly one of the lorries careered across the road, hitting the side of the trap and frightening the pony so much that it shot off down the road breaking the harness and the shafts in the process It all happened so fast that I was still holding the pony's reins and was pulled over the front of the trap, hit the road with a terrific crash and was pulled along the road for several yards before I had the sense or ability to let go. The two occupants in the back of the trap were thrown out and down a twelve-foot slope into a large ditch with about a foot of water in it. I was badly stunned but fortunately was not badly injured with a few cuts and bruises and the other two in the ditch, apart from a soaking, were also very lucky although our clothes looked more of a mess than usual. A jeep came racing up with two officers in it, one of whom fortunately could speak some

English. When the other chaps explained who we were and what we were doing and then showed him what had happened, he immediately walked over to the driver of the lorry involved and, gave him such an almighty punch to the jaw that it knocked him out and he crashed to the ground.

The two officers were so worried about the incident, they kept on apologising and quickly got medical orderlies over to look at our injuries. They were happier when they learned that they were of a minor nature and as some form of compensation they gave us two bottles of schnapps.

Some of the Polish soldiers had been sent to catch and return the pony and when they had they were made to repair the harness and shafts of the trap. By this time the pony had been calmed down and was put back into harness and we were able to continue our journey, only this time I was resting as a passenger in the back of the trap.

This nasty accident had cost us about two hours delay altogether but we still proceeded down the road at a leisurely pace until we reached a town called Deutsch Krone where we succeeded in finding stabling for the animals and wagons and a large comfortable house for us to sleep in. We decided it was such good accommodation for us all that we should stay for a few days to recover from the accident and the rigours and traumas of the journey thus far. The next day we were joined by two more ex-prisoners which brought the number in our party up to thirteen: Charlie, Paul, Porky and myself who were Englishmen, Bob, Gordon and Andy who were Scotsmen, Les who was a Welshman, Paddy who was of course Irish, Bill, the New Zealander, Ed and Min the Americans and Gaud a Frenchman.

Behind the house we had moved into was a large lake and on one eventful day two of the lads found a rowing boat and decided to spend a nice relaxing day boating while the rest of us sunbathed on the grassy banks of the lake.

Suddenly we were startled by a loud bang and we sat up, looked around and saw that on the opposite side of the lake two Russians had started firing a bazooka and it seemed that they thought the rowing boat would make a good target. Charlie said, 'Cor blimey, look at the way they're moving! I'd back them against Oxford and Cambridge any time.'

I had to agree with him because the rowing boat was fairly skimming across the water with Gordon pulling the oars in desperation while the rest of us were standing on the bank cheering and shouting encouragement as the bazooka kept on banging away and making splashes which followed the rowing boat all the way back to where we were standing. They crashed into the bank without receiving any hits and the Russians, who had now stopped firing, stood on the opposite side waving as if they thought it had been a huge joke. When Gordon and Bill had recovered and got their breath back the air became blue with bad language and we had quite a job to restrain them and to stop them from going round to confront the Russians. Although we could understand their feelings we thought it would be unwise particularly in view of the fact that the Russians had machine guns as well as the bazooka and we knew from experience that they didn't care who they used them on.

By the time they had calmed them down enough to release them, the rest of us could not contain ourselves any longer and thought it was the funniest thing we had seen for a long time. But needless to say there were no more volunteers to go boating on the lake.

The following day we were wandering round the town looking to scrounge anything worthwhile when we saw some Frenchmen go into a block of flats carrying what appeared to be parcels of food. After reconnoitring we discovered they were living in a first-floor flat and watched several more Frenchmen enter the flats carrying parcels.

We thought Gaud might object to our planned expedition so we left him in the house on guard and after harnessing the horse and wagon we found some suitable pieces of wood to use as weapons and started off back to the flats where we had seen the Frenchmen. Going up to the first floor we broke into a flat and the Frenchmen inside offered little resistance after we managed to convince them that our need was greater than theirs. In any case, in our opinion, it would be small compensation for all the NAAFI stores they had stolen in 1940.

We went downstairs fully laden and loaded the parcels on to the wagon quickly and off we went to our temporary home. That evening we had a really good meal and Bill said, 'Lucky there aren't any frogs' legs else I might have to return them and I'd really hate to give the French anything. Oh sorry Gaud, I forgot you were there, but in any case you're an exception and I'd give you my unwanted frogs' legs any day.'

The next day, leaving extra guards in the house, some of us went off searching round the town again. We came across a museum which we thought might be worth investigating and inside we found a large showcase in which there were jars of coffee beans, cocoa powder and tea amongst the exhibits. Bob said, 'I haven't had a good cup of tea for ages – I wonder what it would taste like.'

Gordon replied, 'Since I can't find any whisky we might as well try the tea.' He broke open the case and took the jar of tea but the contents of the other jars looked so terrible that we left them there. When we got back to the house we had a brew up and although there was a musty tang to it, the tea was recognisable and taking all things into consideration was quite good.

Chapter 17

Encounter With Polish Girls

This daily routine of wandering round the town continued until gradually everyone began to feel restless and the urge to continue our journey became overwhelming. Finally all the group agreed it was time to load the wagons and move on. On 24th March, 1945 we left Deutsch Krone in our usual convoy and travelled about thirty kilometres until we came to a road junction where a Russian military policeman was on traffic control. After a lot of difficulty we managed to explain, mainly by the use of sign language, that we were Allied ex-prisoners of war. He asked us if we wanted food so naturally we said, 'yes', whereupon he strode off, waving his arms for us to follow him, and led us to a large garage.

When he opened the door we were very surprised to see a large cow standing there. We were even more surprised when the policeman pulled out a gun, shot the cow then indicated we could help ourselves to the food he had provided. After recovering from the initial shock we searched an adjoining house and found a large kitchen knife and an old-fashioned tin bath.

One of the lads who professed to have some knowledge of butchery proceeded to cut joints off the cow which were placed in about six inches of water in the bath which was then suspended over a large bonfire we had built in the back garden.

The Russian policeman stood by watching us and he nodded in approval at our every move. As soon as some of the beef was cooked he joined us for an impromptu meal. We stayed in the house and had some more beef before retiring to the bedrooms and because of the good food we had no trouble getting to sleep.

The next morning we said goodbye to our friendly policeman and taking a good supply of the beef with us we started off in our usual order of convoy. We covered about another thirty kilometres and decided to stop for the night in a small village, and while a couple of the lads started preparing an evening meal the rest of us went exploring round the village as usual. Ed, who was a member of the Rangers (American Commandos), and I went into a small house and discovered it was already occupied by two Polish girls. We began chatting them up as if we were in a dance hall back home and everything seemed to be going fine until my ego was shattered and my ardour rapidly dissipated when one of the girls said, 'English and American men are so slow. If you were Russian or German you would have had us lying on the bed long ago and it would probably have been all over by now'.

I said to Ed, 'Apart from the insult it sounds as if half of the Russian and German Armies have enjoyed themselves with these two. I don't want anything to do with them I'm going back to the lads. Although I tried my best to persuade him to return with me and despite all my warnings of the danger of VD or other diseases he said, 'Well I don't care. Its been such a long time since I've been with a woman, I'm going to stay and if necessary I will stay all night to prove an American can make love better than any Russian or German.'

I left him there and rejoined the others telling them what had happened and since nobody wanted to run the risk of VD there were no volunteers to go and join Ed.

Ed returned the next morning with such a satisfied look on his face that he looked just like the cat who had stolen the cream. 'You should have stayed with me. I had a great time with the girls but it was quite a struggle to keep up with them both on my own,' he said.

Charlie, rather unkindly replied, 'You may not be so happy and smug in about a week's time when you start feeling the pain and itching from a dose,' which immediately wiped the smile from Ed's face as he started worrying and imagining all sorts of things including a strong feeling of itching around his private parts.

We packed up and left that village to continue our journey until we reached the outskirts of a town called Woldenberg and were passing some houses which had been practically destroyed by shelling and bombing when we saw in one of the gardens a couple of bodies.

When we got down to investigate we discovered they were young girls aged about fourteen who had obviously been raped, presumably by several Russian soldiers, and then left to die. Although we had seen many horrific sights since the beginning of the war there is no doubt that the sight of these two poor battered bodies shocked us more than anything we had seen before. We carefully wrapped the bodies in some sheets we had found in one of the houses and buried them together in a shallow grave which we marked with a wooden cross crudely made by tying two pieces of wood together.

It was 26th March and we had travelled about 550 kms from Danzig and in the centre of Woldenberg we came across some Russians who appeared to be in some sort of transport office so we thought it would be a good idea if we could arrange transport on a lorry because this would undoubtedly speed up our journey home. However since we could not speak Russian we were unable to make them understand what we wanted, although strangely enough we had not encountered such problems before and in desperation one of the lads suggested we try them with German. Then all Hell broke loose because these stupid Russians thought we were Germans.

While a couple of the lads tried to get the misunderstanding sorted out I was watching some other Russians who were checking some captured Germans. I noticed that the first thing they did was to make the Germans strip to the waist and raise their arms above their heads whereupon the Russians checked carefully under their arms for any signs of a tattooed number and I saw them find one. Without any further ado a Russian pulled out his revolver and shot the German in the back of his head and then turned to the next German in line and continued his search. Any numbers tattooed under their arms was indisputable proof that they were members of the SS.

Eventually our own problem was sorted out when a Russian officer who could speak some English arrived and after a discussion he told us that if we went down the road for about a mile we would see a lorry park and we could get transport there. We arrived at the lorry park and were very surprised to find some other ex-prisoners there and we got confirmation that transport would be available. After we managed to find some civilians who promised to look after them, we said a rather emotional farewell to our animals and clambered on board a lorry to continue our journey eastwards.

The first town we went through was called Friedenberg and very shortly afterwards we arrived at a town called Bellenchin where to our great delight and surprise we were able to indulge in a hot bath.

After the almost forgotten luxury of a hot bath we were given new underwear and after this second pleasurable treat we had another lovely surprise when we were escorted to a restaurant where we had a very reasonable meal. We were then issued with registration cards and taken to various houses to spend the night in relative comfort. In the morning we had a good breakfast in the same restaurant and clambered on to lorries to continue our journey which took us through Landsburg to a town called Posen. (By now our numbers had increased to almost ninety, all of us ex-prisoners of war of different nationalities.)

This town had suffered the worst damage of any town we had seen so far and whole streets of houses had been flattened to the ground, which made us realise why we had heard the name of Posen so often in the news whenever the fighting on the Eastern Front had been mentioned.

We continued our journey all through the night without any food or stops at all until eventually after a very uncomfortable trip of about two hundred kilometres we finally arrived at Warsino (Wreschen). It was 28th March and we were about 1,000 kms from Danzig and we were given a bowl of soup and a small piece of bread and then we had to climb into cattle trucks in which were some straw palliasses and pillows covered with cotton pillow cases. The train started off and soon picked up speed which it maintained on a journey which took us through Kenin, Kulo, Lowicz, Warsaw and Praga.

The next day we were held up for hours in a station at Katuszyn Siedlice until eventually we began a slow journey through the countryside. After another night of fitful sleep during which we went through Lukow to Brest Litowsky and we stopped all day and were given a bowl of soup and some bread.

We finally left that night at ten o'clock and after another stop-start journey we arrived at a place called Kowel at seven in the morning of 31st March only to find that we had to spend another boring day in a railway station. The usual bowl of soup and small piece of bread was issued and then began a real comedy episode when they pushed the train into a siding and manoeuvred to get another engine on to the front of our train in place of the engine that had pulled our train for all of the journey until now. I don't know why it was thought necessary to change the engines but it provided us with some entertainment while they kept on getting into a terrible mess until eventually they were successful and we finally left with a new engine pulling the train.

At eight o'clock the next morning we arrived at a place called Dubno and realised it was 1st April, but by now we were so bored with the long journey that in the mood we were in, we would have killed anyone making any practical jokes. We left again at nine o'clock and the train began travelling very fast with few stops. When it did occasionally stop in the middle of nowhere we usually took the opportunity to answer the call of nature, but we had to be very alert because the train was apt to start off very suddenly without any warning causing us to make a frantic dash to climb back into the trucks. From our experience of the Russians so far I began to suspect that they thought it was a huge joke to start off without any warning then they would be laughing their heads off whilst watching us making a frantic dash for the train, still struggling to adjust our clothing.

Quite often during these stops in the countryside the peasant farmers came across the fields to the train and we bartered everything we could lay our hands on, including the palliasses and pillow cases, for bread and eggs because we were very hungry.

Eventually this part of our journey ended when we reached a small town called Berditshew where we stopped for a few hours and we were told that we were about seventy kilometres from the seaport of Odessa.

Chapter 18
Arrival in Odessa

Early the next morning, which was the 3rd April, after a journey of about 2,200 kms from Danzig we arrived at Odessa. Waiting to greet us on the platform were three British Army Officers who stared at us as we stepped down on to the platform because most of us were only wearing a pair of underpants, having swapped everything else for food on the journey. After the initial shock had worn off and we had explained the reason for our lack of clothes, they still did not appear to understand why we had done it – probably because they have never known real hunger. In any case we were not the slightest bit interested in their reaction.

We were formed up in some semblance of order outside the railway station and started to march through the town of Odessa. I am sure that even in wartime we would have qualified for one of the strangest groups of soldiers. We certainly got some strange looks, but even we were very surprised when a rather brassy looking woman called out, 'Hello sailor! Have you got any cigarettes to give me for a good time?' There were many catcalls and obscene remarks from us but I cannot imagine where she thought we were hiding the cigarettes.

Eventually we arrived at a very large house to be greeted in the hall by the marvellous sight of British Red Cross ladies who were dispensing cups of tea, bars of Cadbury chocolate, English newspapers dated 4th March, new underwear and cigarettes. For some absurd reason we were separated from the Americans in the same house, and when we had come so far across Russia and shared so many adventures together, it seemed totally unnecessary.

The next day was a return to something vaguely resembling army discipline but after such a long time as prisoners of war when we had spent years doing our utmost to frustrate the discipline of the Germans, we were still inclined to be rebellious and undisciplined. We were issued with new uniforms and received a further issue of biscuits, chocolate and cigarettes from the lovely Red Cross ladies.

The morning afterwards a party of us was taken on lorries to the harbour where we helped unload bales of clothing from a ship on to lorries. There were several American Liberty ships moored alongside the docks and several more were anchored a short distance out in the harbour. When we arrived back at the house we again received a supply of goodies from the Red Cross ladies whilst the Russians started giving us the usual soup and black bread. We could also go into the back garden to get buckets of tea; if you were very lucky you also got a small piece of lemon but nobody was lucky enough to get any milk or sugar. That evening we went into a very large room on the ground floor and watched a show performed by an opera singer, violinist and several dancers. Rather surprisingly I found it very enjoyable although I would have expected it to be too highbrow for my usual tastes.

The next day in addition to the usual issue from the Red Cross ladies, we were given medal ribbons and later escorted to a cinema in the town where much to our disgust we were treated to a showing of a blatant propaganda film extolling the virtues of communism, but fortunately it was only a short film and was followed by a film starring Jan Kiepura which contained some popular songs and excellent singing. The Americans left during the day to embark and I was sorry to see them leave as we had gone through such a lot together and become very good friends. It would not have been so bad if we had been leaving Russia at the same time but for them to go and leave us in Odessa somehow made it seem much worse.

We now settled into a routine for cleaning our room in the morning, receiving our usual supply of goodies and then being free to spend a lot of time lounging about talking about our wartime experiences, where we had been in Europe and how we had been captured. We also talked about our families at home and our plans for the future, but inevitably it wasn't long before reaction set in and it started to become very monotonous and boring. One afternoon we went upstairs to a large room which had been converted to a cinema and watched a film called Hurricane; I cannot remember what it was about but at least it passed some time. When we returned downstairs we heard that the American ships were still anchored in the harbour and nobody had any idea why their sailing had been delayed.

Ever since our arrival in Odessa the house we were in had been guarded by armed Russian soldiers and we could never figure out whether this was to keep us in or to keep the Russian civilians out. One evening the monotony and perpetual boredom overcame us and we decided to find out whether our past experience would be sufficient to get us out of the house and past the guards. So at about ten o'clock we crept out to the back garden, clambered over heaps of rubble without making any noise and then climbed over the surrounding wall without being detected by the guards.

The nine escapees, namely Charlie, Paul, Porky, Bob, Gordon, Andy, Les, Paddy and myself, wandered towards what we thought was the centre of town and we came across what was obviously some sort of night club.

We went down a flight of stairs and through a small hall into a large smoke-filled room which was crowded mostly with sailors and several women too. Since we had no Russian money to buy drinks with, we offered cigarettes but when they found out who we were they made us sit down at a table and brought several vodkas for us. In one corner of the room a sailor was playing an accordion while another was seated at a piano and knowing that Paddy had a good voice, we persuaded him to stand up and sing. He must have had enough vodkas because he got up without too much argument and got the two musicians to play some music he liked.

When Paddy started to sing all the noise and chatter in the room stopped and the Russians obviously appreciated his singing because they kept on bringing drinks to our table, but unfortunately for Paddy he was too popular for his own good because every time he stopped singing and went to sit down, they grabbed him and persuaded him to continue singing. Naturally we loved his singing more and more as we continued to drink the free vodkas and as a result I lost count of the songs Paddy sang that night and of how many vodkas I had drunk but there is no doubt we had a marvellous time and, with the exception of Paddy, we all got very drunk. (However, between us we could later piece together what happened.)

Sometime in the early hours of the morning we all staggered to our feet and decided it was time for bed so we said our farewells to the sailors and the women and climbed up the stairs to the road. Since Paddy was the only sober one amongst us we relied on him to guide us back to the house. When we arrived it was impossible for us to climb back over the wall in our condition so we went to the front entrance but the guards refused to let us in. As we had nowhere else to go we just stood there singing except Paddy who had lost his voice from his previous efforts.

We were creating so much noise and disturbing all the other occupants that after a time a British officer came out and persuaded the guards to let us in. To say the officer was annoyed must be the understatement of the year because he was absolutely fuming and I don't know whether this was because we had disturbed him or because he had not had all the drinks that we had had.

Because of the state that we were in, his shouting had little effect and was just being submerged by our singing. Charlie must have heard what he said though because he suddenly said, 'Why don't you put us all in the cooler then – it will be just like old times!' Either the officer didn't hear him or chose to ignore him and after a lot more shouting and arm-waving he succeeded in quietening us down enough to inform us that he would consider our extremely bad behaviour in the morning and decide on an appropriate punishment. Then we turned round and staggered off to our beds.

In the morning we all woke up with thick heads and it wasn't until mid-morning that we realised Paddy was missing and we searched the house from top to bottom. After some discussion it emerged that nobody had seen Paddy since we had stood outside the house singing the previous night but we decided it would probably be better if we kept quiet and waited to see if he turned up.

The officer came into our room and warned us that he would overlook our disgusting behaviour this time but any future incidents of that nature would be severely punished. He refused to believe my story that a gang of Russian sailors had kidnapped us and taken us to a strange night club and of how we had tried unsuccessfully for hours to escape; he even had this stupid idea that we had drunk that horrible vodka willingly he just looked at me and said, 'This is not a joke and I am warning you: don't try my patience any further!'

I thought it would be wise to keep quiet and he went away. Shortly after this little confrontation we got our usual rations of chocolate and cigarettes but there was still no sign of Paddy and although we were getting very worried we decided it would still be best to keep quiet. The American ships sailed that day which increased our feelings of frustration and depression, partly because our American friends had actually gone and partly because there was no news of a ship for us. But shortly afterwards we cheered up a bit when they issued us with embarkation tickets and after a lot of argument we managed to get one for Paddy.

After we had finished cleaning the room the next morning we received our usual rations but to our surprise we were also given some medical parcels containing vitamins etc. and for the first time they introduced communal eating. We all had to go to a large room on the ground floor where I met Alan, an American who had just arrived, and we had quite a long chat and got very friendly.

That evening, much to our surprise and relief, Paddy returned and he told us how when he had been walking back from the night club a young woman had spoken to him and walked back with him to the house. Whilst all the noise and argument was going on she had persuaded him to take her home and I thought it was amazing that we hadn't noticed at the time. It just goes to show how drunk we must have been.

Paddy said he had fallen in love with her and had only come back to get a supply of chocolate and cigarettes and then was returning to her house. We tried our best to dissuade him but he was so determined that it was no use. In the end we gave him a good supply of chocolate bars and cigarettes and helped him to get away from the house without the guards or any officers seeing him.

Next morning after we had finished the cleaning we did a few exercises, then got our usual rations and went downstairs for a meal; I must say that the food had improved with communal eating and after the meal I went upstairs with Al and the rest of our gang where we had a lively singsong.

We heard some strong rumours that British ships had entered the harbour but we could not get any confirmation of this so our frustration continued. After the usual routine the next morning we were entertained by a group of opera singers and again this music was not really my cup of tea although at least it gave us a break from the usual monotonous routine and it helped pass some time. But it was obvious that the waiting and soul-destroying monotony was beginning to affect us all. The next few days continued with no break except for a couple of films and some long discussions on a multitude of subjects.

Any further excursions to night clubs were ruled out mainly because the armed guards had been supplemented by dog patrols which to us seemed rather unfriendly behaviour towards allies, and also because without Paddy such an excursion lost its appeal.

However, much to our surprise and delight Larry and Doug turned up and we had a great reunion and exchanged news of what had happened to each of us since we were last together.

15th April dawned and turned out to be the day we had been longing for because during the morning we were told to pack our belongings (which mostly consisted of chocolate bars and cigarettes) into our newly issued kitbags and prepare to go to the harbour. Much to our surprise Paddy chose this day to come for some more chocolate and cigarettes but this time, after a *lot* of persuasion, we managed to get him to agree to return home with us.

We got the distinct impression that despite his loud protestations that he loved her and what a lovely clean woman she was and what a lovely home she had, the initial pleasure and bloom had gone from the relationship and this had helped change his mind so that he was now reconciled to coming to the harbour with us.

I said goodbye to Al who was going to have to wait for an American ship and we left the house at about five o'clock in the evening for our much-longed for journey home. Although at times it had seemed much longer, we had in fact been in Odessa for only twelve days during which time there had been a steady flow of ex-prisoners who had either escaped or been liberated by the Russians, so that there were now about four hundred of us who went to the harbour to board the passenger liner *Nieuw Amsterdam*.

Chapter 19

Journey Home at Last

We were allocated to different mess halls and after settling in had an excellent meal after which there was a lot of hilarity as we tried to get into and make ourselves comfortable in hammocks. Some of the chaps finished up underneath the hammock, madly clinging on and trying to get back on top. I was certainly in no position to criticise or to give advice as I was getting into a worse state than anyone, and in the end most people finished up sleeping on the mess tables or on the floor.

The next morning got off to a wonderful start with kippers for breakfast washed down with the best tea I had tasted for years (literally). At about ten in the morning the ship sailed from Odessa and the brilliant sunshine seemed like a good omen, as if the sun was wishing us Godspeed.

The food continued to be excellent and the taste of the beautiful white bread was particularly memorable as we had only had black bread for such a long time. In fact it was nearly five years since I had tasted white bread. Later we went into the cinema to watch a film called '*One Hundred Men and a Girl*' starring Deanna Durbin. We were issued with new underwear, shirt, socks and a cap, and after a lovely hot shower I went for a medical and was passed fit although like all the ex-prisoners I was still undernourished.

Although Paddy had continually told us about the lovely clean woman he had spent that time with in Odessa, his medical revealed that she had given him a dose of VD and he was immediately put on a course of drugs.

Soldiers being what they are, he came in for a lot of rude and obscene remarks and we rather unkindly kept on saying that we knew now from what he had told us that there were such lovely clean women in Odessa.

In the afternoon we anchored in Istanbul harbour. The scenery and the skyline of minarets provided a fantastic backdrop to the harbour and during this stay we were given an advance of pay of five pounds which we were able to spend in the ship's shop. We left Istanbul on 18th April at ten in the morning and we saw a film called, 'Phantom Lady' In the late afternoon I was issued with a Royal Navy duffle coat and detailed to carry out a duty as gun watch so I happened to be on deck when we passed the monument at Dardenelles which I thought beautiful and very impressive.

The next morning I was again on duty as gun watch from eight until noon and it was during this watch that we passed Crete and Greece and with the weather getting noticeably warmer we could now start enjoying sessions of sunbathing on the deck. I went to the cinema the next day and saw a good film called 'Calling Dr Gillespie' and afterwards settled down to write some letters home. We went through the Straits of Messina and saw Mount Etna and the coast of Sicily.

It was now 21st April and a beautiful Saturday morning when we passed Mount Vesuvius at seven o'clock and docked in Naples harbour at about eight that morning. We were visited by Red Cross officials and several British Army officers among whom was a Lieutenant Colonel from the KRRC who were all very friendly, chatting and asking us if we were all right. A RAF dance band with guest artists including a Cockney comedian came aboard and gave us a good show and the next day we were entertained by the band of the 7th Devons followed by the Red Cross feeding us with tea and cakes. Later the RAF band returned with Patricia Burke and put on another very good show for us.

I had a long chat with an army captain who had come aboard and inquired about my eldest brother Ted who was serving with the 14th Army in Burma. Although obviously he could not give me specific information about my brother he did give me all the latest news from that area. We were given copies of the *Union Jack* and the *Stars and Stripes* as well as magazines which helped us to catch up on some of the news to pass the time. On the following Monday we were entertained by a US army band and a concert party gave us a good show. Afterwards we received an issue of pipes and pipe tobacco which made a change from cigarettes but I found it very difficult to get used to a pipe and it didn't seem to give me the same satisfaction as cigarettes.

On Tuesday, 24th April, troops from the Italian Front were embarking to go home on leave along with a few Wrens and an ENSA concert party. We were given another two pounds advance pay but by this time the ship was packed to capacity and we didn't like this at all; although we didn't begrudge the troops their leave it did mean that we were very cramped and no longer had the run of the ship and the luxury of plenty of space.

After leaving Naples the weather got very humid and uncomfortable and before very long we were again bored with the monotony. There was some excitement created when horse races were organised on deck and Wrens came round selling race cards. Since we had not had any opportunity to talk with attractive young English ladies for many years (I have no wish to detract from the lovely Red Cross ladies but even they would admit they were a bit mature for us), we naturally wanted at least a conversation with some of them. Unfortunately they made it abundantly clear that we were too lowly and they even ignored our polite good-mornings.

Charlie in particular took exception to the way the Wrens had behaved and had on numerous occasions totally ignored him, so when a Wren offered him a race card and said they were sixpence each, Charlie lost his temper 'Doesn't fucking cost much to speak to a stuck-up cow like you does it!' he said and he walked away leaving the Wren very shocked and embarrassed.

We all understood and could sympathise with Charlie's outburst because we had all suffered the same snubs from the Wrens and in fact none of the ex-prisoners would buy a race card.

The next day we were issued with shoes, shorts and socks and we also had another full medical inspection. At about seven in the evening we sighted the coast of Spain and at eight we arrived at Gibraltar. During the night our sleep was disturbed by the constant dropping of depth charges from motor launches which continued until daybreak. We spent another day in Gibraltar harbour, then at seven in the evening left in a convoy consisting of sixteen merchant ships with several of them carrying troops, two tugs and five destroyers.

The sea began to get much rougher and several of the chaps were seasick but fortunately it did not affect me and I spent most of that day, 30th April, sitting on deck chatting to others who were also lucky enough to be unaffected by the movement of the ship. We had to make sure we were well protected from the wind and to make certain that those who were being sick knew which side of the ship to go and hang over.

As I was unaffected by the weather I had to take a turn at being a mess orderly the next morning, and as the sea got even rougher the number wanting any food reduced dramatically which made my job much easier. The number of seasick sufferers kept on increasing but nevertheless everybody without exception had to queue to get a vaccination in the arm. Fortunately my luck was still holding out because even this jab did not affect me.

We woke up to very strong winds and torrential rain so we all had to stay below in the crowded conditions. With nearly everybody smoking heavily the atmosphere was appalling, ten times worse than a London 'pea souper' with everyone coughing and spluttering their heads off. There wasn't much that could be done to ease the situation unless everybody stopped smoking and I for one was not brave enough to suggest it, particularly as I wanted to continue smoking as well. Since the arrival of the troops on board the Army discipline had increased to the extent that there were separate toilets for officers, warrant officers, NCOs and at the end of the line there were toilets for other ranks.

Because of the large number of 'other ranks' it worked out that there were far fewer toilets which of course resulted in long queues. This overcrowding was the direct cause of a very nasty incident which involved one of the ex-prisoners, a young Scottish lad, who had had a particularly rough time in Germany. The aftermath of that experience combined with the very rough seas was causing him to feel unwell, and at this particular moment his stomach was misbehaving. He went to the 'other ranks' toilets which of course were full with a long queue waiting outside so in desperation he went into the warrant officers' toilets which were empty. But unfortunately a warrant officer caught him when he was coming out and shouted at him, 'You know you shouldn't use these toilets. Oh I recognise you now – you're one of those undisciplined bastards who have been sitting on your arses in Germany enjoying yourselves whilst we've been fighting the war for you. Report to the Orderly Officer at nine in the morning – you're on a charge!'

The young Scotsman still feeling under the weather staggered back to our mess deck and told us what had happened and what the Warrant Officer had said. The story quickly spread amongst the ex-prisoners who went berserk and even I heard some new swear words. They quickly decided that, regardless of the consequences, they would find the Warrant Officer and punish him. Even although none of us were fully fit I think our anger more than made up for any lack of fitness.

Several groups of us started to search the ship and after about an hour without any success we heard a voice come over the tannoy. 'This is the OC Troops with a very important and special message to all ex-prisoners on board. I have been informed about the unfortunate instance that occurred a short while ago and can only apologise for the stupid remarks and insults that the Warrant Officer in question made. I would ask you all to return to your mess deck immediately as I can assure you that you will not be allowed to find him as I have him under armed guard and intend to keep him like that until we reach Liverpool and I give you my word he will receive suitable punishment.'

We all knew it would be pointless to continue searching for the WO so we returned to our mess deck but the general opinion was that WO Martin was a very lucky man regardless of what punishment he may receive in England because at least he would still be alive whereas if we the ex-prisoners had found him there is no doubt that he would have gone overboard.

The anger and excitement caused by this incident gradually died down and the weather was at last becoming calmer. Although it was still drizzling we managed to watch a Sunderland flying boat patrolling over the convoy for hours. We had a concert and some community singing but the monotony of the long trip was giving me depression again. The next day the drizzly weather continued but the news that General Eisenhower had announced that German troops were surrendering in large numbers did cheer us up a bit.

At last we docked in Liverpool and all the troops going home on leave from Italy were disembarking while we hung over the side watching and wondering why we weren't going down the gangway as well.

Despite our very careful scrutiny of all the troops going down the gangway we didn't see WO Martin and we never did manage to find out what happened to him.

That evening we sailed from Liverpool and some wit said, 'We're now going on a sunshine cruise of the Mediterranean to recover from the long trip,' and was hit by a multitude of missiles. Shortly afterwards we were told that we were bound for Glasgow and indeed after a fairly short journey we sailed up the Clyde at eight in the morning of Saturday 5th May and we finally docked at five o'clock in the evening. As soon as we were tied up some Red Cross personnel came aboard and issued us with cigarettes and sweets and I was able to send a telegram to my mother.

A message came over the Tannoy informing us that we would be staying on board until Monday morning when we would be going non-stop on a train to Sussex. Doug said to me, 'I only live a mile away – I can't stay on board here all weekend and then go all the way to Sussex without seeing my family when I'm right on the doorstep. To hell with all this rubbish! I'm going to try and get off the ship and go home, do you want to come with me?' 'Well I'll only be bored stiff if I stay here so I'm game. Yes okay, I'll come with you let's have a look round,' I replied.

There was a guard on duty at the bottom of the gangway so we made our way to the stern of the ship where we found a long rope in a locker, tied it to the rail and with great difficulty managed to get down it to the quayside.

It was dusk by now and we quickly got behind a stack of crates and then slowly made our way along the dockside away from the guard and the ship until we could get behind some customs sheds. Eventually we reached a wall, climbed over it and then dropped to the pavement outside the dockyard.

It was, of course, the first time for nearly five years that either of us had set foot on a pavement in the United Kingdom so it was a very emotional moment for us both. It took Doug a little while to get his bearings but then we went rushing down the road like a couple of kids just let out of school. It seemed like just a few seconds before he stopped outside of a large block of flats and said 'Well this is it, Home Sweet Home. I live on the first floor – let's go up and find out if there is anyone at home!'

We went upstairs and he knocked on a door which was opened by his father. The look of astonishment on his face was really something to behold as he grabbed hold of Doug and said, 'Oh God is it really you, Dougie after all this time. Tell me I'm not dreaming.' Then at the top of his voice he shouted, 'Hey quick, come and look everybody. Dougie has come home at last!' Dougie's mother and his sister quickly appeared and there was a lot of kissing and hugging, with all of them crying their eyes out, while I was just stood there feeling a bit embarrassed by it all.

At last Dougie turned round to me and said, 'This is a pal of mine. We've been through a lot together. Then we were both dragged into the living room and told to sit down and make ourselves comfortable. I cannot remember in which order or how much but we certainly consumed a hell of a lot of tea and whisky that night. When everything had settled down a bit, Doug managed to explain about the ship and our escape from it which created lots of laughter. He also told them about some of our other experiences, but only the good times.

Naturally there was endless catching-up with family news since Doug had left home. Suddenly his father said, 'I must go and fetch Uncle Bob,' and he went out and returned about half an hour later with Uncle Bob and several other relatives who between them had thoughtfully brought a good supply of whisky.

After we had had a meal and a few more drinks, the flat was getting crowded with more family and friends including a piper in full dress-uniform. What with the Piper and plenty of whisky, the singing and dancing attracted all the other residents and neighbours in the flats and although I suppose a lot of them never knew what the celebration was all about they didn't hesitate to join in and even the stairways became crowded with people singing and dancing.

Some time during the night I passed out and don't remember anything more until I woke up on the sofa with the sun streaming through the window on to my face. I moved to get away from the glare in my eyes but this sudden movement woke up a little man who began banging a hammer in my head. It was at this point that an angel of mercy in the shape of Doug's mother appeared with a cup of tea and a couple of aspirins. After taking this life-saver I managed to open my eyes to look round the room. Every table and surface appeared to be covered with empty whisky bottles, dirty glasses and overflowing ashtrays which seemed proof that everybody had been having a good time.

Soon after breakfast of a few cups of tea, I was persuaded to go for a walk with Doug. He took me to a nearby park where he pointed out all the things which meant so much to him, in particular the football pitches where he used to play. When we returned the afternoon was mostly spent with the family catching up on all the details of Dougie's experiences during the five years he had been away and, of course, Doug was anxious to find out what had been happening here in Glasgow, particularly to his family. Eventually, I think they all got the news they wanted.

After tea there was a repeat performance of the previous evening's party which again seemed to go on forever with an endless supply of whisky. Early the next morning Doug's mother woke me up again with a cup of tea and aspirins but this time she said, 'You have to get up quickly. Doug said you've got to hurry back to the ship in time to collect your belongings and catch the train.'

After snatching a very hurried breakfast there were some tearful goodbyes and I thanked Doug's family for making me so welcome and Doug and I walked quickly back to the docks where we decided that in our hung-over state the wall would be too much so we went to the nearest gate and after a lot of argument the policeman there let us through. We walked along the quayside to the ship and found the band of the Argyll and Sutherland Highlanders playing on the dockside and Doug said, 'Now isn't that good of them to arrange for a Highland Band to be here especially to pipe us on board.'

After another argument with a guard, a warrant officer appeared and after he had recovered from what seemed like an attack of apoplexy when he heard our story, he took us back on board.

When we got on board he took us in front of the OC Troops who fortunately saw the funny side of things and said, 'Well I can hardly give you jankers [extra fatigues] or confine you to barracks because we're due to leave in about an hour. You had better go and pack but make sure you behave yourselves in future or you may not be so lucky again.'

We went below to our mess deck and told the rest of the lads about the great time we had had and they were absolutely livid because we had not invited them to join us. We just ignored their complaints and started our packing.

The Band continued to play while the ex-prisoners went down the gangway. For a large proportion of them it was the first time for about five years that they had set foot in the United Kingdom and Doug and I knew they must have been feeling just as emotional as we had the Saturday before. Several warrant officers appeared and rather stupidly tried to bring some discipline into the proceedings. Eventually they did succeed in getting us into a large customs shed but their attempts to get us lined up in any semblance of order was not very successful. A small party of officers arrived and among them was a brigadier from the War Office in London who was helped on to a crate while the warrant officers shouted at us to stand to attention. The Brigadier smiled at us and rather unnecessarily I thought told us to stand at ease despite the fact that nobody had taken any notice of the warrant officers' orders to stand to attention. He then proceeded to make what I think was intended to be a welcome home speech but for the majority of us it was boring, irrelevant and, what made it worse, he gave the impression that he was making the speech because it was part of his duties and not because he meant any of the sentiments he was expressing or had any feelings for us or the fact that we had been away from home for such a long time.

It appeared as if we had all come to the same conclusion at exactly the same time because we decided we had heard enough, turned round and ignoring the Brigadier started to walk out of the customs shed towards the train. Despite shouts and threats by the warrant officers we continued walking to the railway platform where NAAFI girls were handing out mugs of tea, chocolate, cigarettes, packed sandwiches and newspapers for our journey.

Mind you it took some persuading to get the lads to leave the girls alone before eventually we all got on the train which finally left at eleven o'clock. For all that we cared, the Brigadier could have still been on his crate talking to himself in the customs shed because we never saw him or any of the warrant officers again. The first town we could definitely identify as we went through it at about five in the evening was Newcastle and all along the route there were crowds of people waving to us and cheering, and in some cases waving banners proclaiming victory. At about two in the morning we reached Clapham Junction and not long afterwards Haywards Heath where we got off the train. We were directed through the station to a fleet of lorries parked in the station yard and told to climb aboard and after a short journey we arrived at a camp composed of large marquees. After a full medical inspection, we were directed to another marquee to get new uniforms, railway warrants, papers and an advance of pay.

Then somebody shouted that it was VE Day and the War in Europe was over at last. We all shouted, 'We've won at last! Wish we could see the faces of those German bastards now!' Above all though, there was a huge feeling of relief and all we wanted was to get home to celebrate with our families. Everybody was talking at once and it was obvious that we were all so excited and happy that at long last our dream had come true. Unfortunately we were still unable to celebrate properly.

The personnel in the camp were trying to process everybody as quickly as they could. Eventually we were persuaded to go to another marquee, and because we were so tired from the long train journey and the inspections followed by all the excitement, everyone managed to fall asleep on the camp beds.

It seemed as if we had hardly lain down before we were called for breakfast, during which we were of course talking about the exciting news of victory in Europe.

After breakfast we collected our belongings and were taken to the railway station where we caught a train to

Clapham Junction. During the journey we discussed our future plans and everyone was keen to keep in touch.

When we came into the station where we were going to split up to head for our homes in various parts of the country, we were shaking hands and hugging each other. It was a very emotional moment. Although we were now tough old veterans, there were hints of tears and though we wanted to get on our way, we were reluctant to say goodbye. Those who disembarked left the train with shouts of, 'Don't forget to write!'

At Victoria Station there were some more emotional farewells and most went to the Underground to continue their journeys. As I walked across the station I felt strangely alone and sad. I particularly thought of Doug and the other Scotsmen with whom I had experienced so much.

I stood outside the Grosvenor Hotel where I knew the bus stop was for the Number Eleven. When I got on the bus I was astonished to see a lady conductress on the platform since I had never seen one in England before. She looked at me and said, 'Who do you think you're staring at?'

I blushed and mumbled something and then asked for a penny fare to Stanley Bridge. She burst out laughing and said, 'Where have you been hiding? It's been a fourpenny fare for ages now.'

When I told her that I had been away for five years and that she was the first lady conductress I had seen she said, 'Oh well, never mind the fare love. Give us a kiss,' and she grabbed me and gave me a big kiss.

After giving me such a pleasant and unexpected welcome back to London, she had to go and collect other fares. I spent the rest of the journey staring out of the window at the bomb-damaged buildings. Despite the damage I was able to recognise many familiar landmarks along the King's Road.

When I got off the bus at Stanley Bridge I called out, 'Cheerio', to the conductress. She replied, 'Good luck soldier. You can travel on my bus anytime!'

I managed to find the place where my mother had been forced to move after our home was destroyed by a land-mine. It was a small flat in a side street just over the boundary in Fulham.

When mother opened the door and saw me I thought she was going to faint and I grabbed hold of her. We hugged and kissed and both of us started crying.

It seemed as if she didn't want me to let go in case I disappeared again but eventually we went inside and sat down. She made some tea and saying all the time how much she had missed and worried about me.

When we were drinking our tea she told me that she was sorry but Lilian had married a Yank. This news came as a great shock to me as I had been engaged to Lilian since the early part of the war and had received letters as normal until shortly before leaving Danzig.

My mother was very upset at having to be the bearer of bad news on such an otherwise happy occasion so I had to put on a brave face and said, 'Oh well, maybe it's better that I didn't know before. I wouldn't have liked to have received a "Dear John" letter while I was still a prisoner. Let's try and forget it. I'm home and safe with you and that's the most important thing.'

Chapter 20

Where the Heart Is

The first evening back home I took mother to visit the Herbert family who had been our neighbours for many years before the war. We had a marvellous time drinking and reminiscing about the old days when we all lived in the same block of flats in Chelsea and of course of catching up on all the news of what had happened to both families during the war. The next day I went to see Bill Parker's wife, Ann, as I had worked with them both in John Lewis's before the war, but unfortunately she was out so I went and had tea with Helen, my brother George's wife, and discussed the latest news she had from him and what was happening in Normandy.

Later mother and I went to visit my eldest brother's wife, Ivy, who lived about a mile away and she told us the latest news from Ted who was still in Burma. I went up to the West End with Ivy and as we were strolling along Oxford Street it brought back memories of John Lewis's where I had worked as an accounts clerk before the war and it crossed my mind that maybe when I was out of the Army I may go back and work there again.

We walked past Davies Street which brought back memories of the QVR Drill Hall where we had spent many evenings drilling and weapon-training. I noticed Wimpole Street where we had been billeted in a shop in 1939. After we had finished looking round the shops we sent a telegram to Ted who was still with the 14th Army in Burma and caught a bus back to Fulham.

I managed to contact Ann Parker on the telephone and we had a long chat during which she told me how worried she was about Bill because she hadn't received any news of him for some time. I did my best to cheer her up by trying to convince her that he could be turning up on the doorstep any day now.

Afterwards I remember writing to Finsbury Circus to get some clothing coupons and the next day I spent hours writing to my brothers in three different countries. I had not seen Ted or George for five years and I hadn't seen John for about sixteen years; Ted was in Burma, George was in Germany now and John was in New Zealand where he had emigrated to when he was fifteen years old under a Salvation Army scheme.

That evening I went over to Notting Hill to meet Ann and was introduced to her friend Betty and her family, I learnt that Betty had been let down like me but anyway we all went to the local pub and had a really good time.

The next day I went with my sister-in-law Ivy and her younger sister, May, to the shop where Ivy worked and spent some time chatting and sampling some of the delicious cakes. That night I went with Ivy her brother Orry, sister May and her husband Fred and some of their neighbours to the local pub called The Cottage which was near Fulham football ground, Craven Cottage.

I can remember drinking several pints of beer and joining in the singing until the landlord turned us all out at closing time. We staggered back to Ivy's house and at daybreak I was sitting on her doorstep eating huge sandwiches and washing them down with large mugs of tea. These outings became a regular occurrence and I think I probably spent as much time drunk as sober until eventually I was told to report back and I was sent to Great

Missenden on 12th July for a three-week assessment course.

Like many other ex-prisoners at that time I would have welcomed the opportunity to take revenge on the Germans so I volunteered to go to Germany as part of the Occupation Forces but as far as I know none of the ex-prisoners were accepted.

I met many ex-prisoners at Great Missenden but did not meet a single one I had met before. Nevertheless, probably because of our similar experiences, we soon became friends and whenever we could get away in the evenings we used to go to Rickmansworth and have a good time in the pubs getting merry and generally having a good time.

On 18th July I had to go in front of a medical board who re-classified me as B2 which meant that there was a restriction on the type of unit to which I could be posted. The next day I had an interview with a personnel selection officer who told me I would be posted to become a clerk with either the RAOC, RAMC or REME and no amount of pleading or shouting would persuade him to post me to my old regiment. In the end I lost my temper and finished up swearing; and calling him all the names under the sun, then I stormed out of his office, slamming the door behind me. I went back home for a few days until I received official posting papers ordering me to report for duty with the REME Holding Battalion at Woolwich Barracks. I duly reported as ordered, feeling thoroughly depressed and angry that I had been sent to what I regarded, rather unfairly I suppose, as an inferior unit of the Army instead of my own regiment which was a front-line regiment.

I had to report sick with a terrible sore throat and was immediately put into the Royal Herbert Military Hospital where I was told that I had a very bad case of thrush which was apparently a nasty throat infection.

I very soon learnt how Queen Alexandra nurses got their nickname of 'battle-axes', there was no sympathetic treatment or mollycoddling from them. Perhaps it was just as well I could hardly speak else I would have had extreme difficulty controlling my language. The worst of the lot was a real dragon of a ward sister and I doubt whether there were any walking wounded there who had not broken all track records in getting back to their units.

After a week of this imprisonment and constant doses of medicine and tablets, I was discharged and the next day I was posted to Bordon camp in Hampshire. On arrival I discovered there were four hundred ex-prisoners from practically every regiment in the British Army and because we had all been posted to the REME against our wishes we were, as a gesture of defiance, all wearing our own regimental cap badges and a mixture of red, green, black and khaki berets. In a very short time I discovered that there was no barber in the camp so the first thing I did was to go to the orderly room to get a signed pass authorising me to go out of camp to the village. I used to visit the village frequently, supposedly for a haircut.

The original intention was to put all of us through basic training including square bashing (drilling on the parade ground) but after ten days we had succeeded in convincing the authorities that we were untrainable and to try and threaten us with jankers (fatigues) or even the glasshouse (army prison) was a bit stupid and constituted no threat to men like us who had spent up to five years as POWs in Germany. So we got into a routine where if we felt like a bit of exercise we played football, went for a run or on very rare occasions did some physical training.

After a couple of weeks of time-wasting routine, we were joined much to our surprise by fifteen hundred recruits who had just been called up on National Service. Unsuccessful attempts were made to integrate us among them and to start all of us on basic training, but these attempts met with as little success as the first attempt and in fact was even more disastrous because it meant we were able to teach the National Servicemen some very bad habits.

The Commanding Officer came to the same conclusion and decided that it would be far better to concentrate on training the National Servicemen on their own, leaving us to carry on with our own programme as we felt inclined.

Frequently a gang of us used to go to a pub in Bordon village and after consuming a load of beer would stagger back to the camp. On one occasion we gathered up a collection of dustbin lids, a Scotsman produced a set of bagpipes and we proceeded to give an impromptu concert outside the Regimental Sergeant Major's bungalow. It wasn't very long before he made it abundantly clear that he had no ear for music, particularly the sort we were producing, and with discretion being the better part of valour finished off our concert on a very loud high note and we disappeared quickly to our quarters. The next morning the RSM was issuing threats about what would happen if there were any repeat performances. In our room in the barracks we had a very cocky young National Serviceman who occasionally annoyed us but was generally ignored as not being worth the effort to do anything about. However one night when we returned from the pub and noticed him fast asleep on his cot, we all decided to have a bit of fun. We all started shouting, 'Come on, wake up! You're late on parade! Get your full kit on – we're supposed to be going on night manoeuvres.' We shook him and shouted until he jumped out of bed, dressed very quickly, grabbed his rifle and dashed downstairs to the parade ground where he looked round despairingly wondering where the rest of the Battalion was. All the time we were rolling about with laughter. When the penny finally dropped he returned to the room looking very sheepish and upset but there was nothing he could do about it so after about half an hour things settled down and became quiet and we all dropped off to sleep.

I think that experience taught him a valuable lesson because after that he was a bit more subdued and very careful what he said to any ex-prisoner.

Every Friday night most of us used to board a train for London. I used to get off the train at Clapham Junction then caught a train to Wimbledon then transfer to go on the Underground to Fulham Broadway. On arrival there I used to tell the ticket collector that I had got on the train at Wimbledon and had been in too much of a hurry to get a ticket and he seemed to think the sixpence I gave him was more than sufficient to cover the journey.

One Sunday night when we arrived back at Bordon on the late train we discovered there was a welcoming committee of Military Police who wanted to check all weekend passes and to make sure that we had bought the correct tickets. Since the majority of us had neither, we had to attempt to get out of the station without any inspection and this resulted in a direct confrontation with the military police which turned into a nasty fight.

Fortunately I was one of the lucky ones who succeeded in getting past the police and back to camp with only a few cuts and bruises but some were caught and held by the police. We were told that they would have to face charges, especially as several of the policemen had been to hospital for treatment for their injuries which included some broken arms and cracked ribs.

Next morning all of the ex-prisoners not in custody paraded round the camp with large banners demanding that those held should be released immediately. Whether our protest had any effect or not I don't know but all the offenders got off very lightly with sentences of being confined to camp for seven days.

On the following Wednesday night we decided to stay in camp to keep those who were confined company. We went into the NAAFI canteen and stayed there drinking all evening. The more beer that was drunk produced more raucous behaviour until in one corner a chap was playing the piano while several drinkers were attempting to dismantle it, and in another corner a group were having a battle using fire extinguishers and water hoses. I am sorry to say it made a horrible mess of the canteen which did not please the Commanding Officer. The next morning he had us all lined up on the parade ground and said, 'You are a very bad example and influence on the young National Servicemen so I have arranged for sixty of you, whom I consider to be the ringleaders, to go on a course at Arborfield Barracks immediately.'

That same afternoon the sixty 'ringleaders' which for some reason included me, climbed on to lorries with our kitbags to be taken to Arborfield Barracks. When we arrived we were allocated to barrack rooms and told the course would start at nine o'clock promptly the next morning.

We duly reported to the lecture room and were told by a young warrant officer, who we thought was probably a National Serviceman, that we had better behave ourselves, must only wear a REME cap badge and must always appear fully and smartly dressed. He wouldn't stand for any nonsense or indiscipline. We were going to be given an advanced course in clerical procedures and typewriting which would last for six weeks. His attitude didn't go down too well with the lads and the prospect of the course with the added pleasure of being continually nagged at by him was not at all attractive so there was a unanimous decision that we should cause as many problems as possible as often as we could.

Whether the warrant officer and the other instructors fully realised what we were up to or whether they thought we were all stupid wasn't clear but five days later we were paraded on the square and the Commanding Officer said he thought (and all the instructors agreed with him) that it was a waste of everybody's time keeping us there so we would be returned to Bordon camp first thing the next day.

We duly arrived back at Bordon camp the next day and were immediately lined up again on the parade ground.

We had only just got into lines when the most unhappy looking commanding officer I have ever seen said, 'That was supposed to be a six weeks course – what on earth happened there?' One wit shouted out, 'We couldn't bear to be away from you and the Sergeant Major for such a long time and we thought you were missing us.' The CO said, 'Shut up in the ranks, you can be sure we do not want you and I intend to get you all posted away from here as soon as possible. In the meantime keep away from the National Servicemen and behave yourselves.'

By this time I was absolutely fed up with the Army so I asked for an interview with the CO and made a request for a compassionate release on the grounds that my mother was alone and since she had been bombed out of her home she had been very nervous and suffering from depression, especially at night, so she really needed me at home to look after her. The CO promised to forward my request as soon as possible but in the meantime, true to what he had said on the parade ground, he quickly arranged postings for a large number of us, and I was being posted to a REME unit at Putney.

Since there were no clerical vacancies in this unit I was detailed for duties in the officers' mess which was in a boathouse on the side of the River Thames opposite Craven Cottage where in the past I had spent many happy hours on the terraces. My mother only lived a short distance away so I applied for and succeeded in getting a living-out pass, which meant that every afternoon I finished my duties and took a leisurely stroll along the river bank and over Putney Bridge and along New Kings Road to home.

As an added bonus, because I was living at home, I received a living-out allowance and obviously working in the officers mess meant I had easy access to first-class food supplies. The experience of scrounging things in Germany, or to put it another way, appropriating any articles left lying about which would be helpful to my well-being made sure that our larder was kept well stocked.

I had forgotten all about my application for compassionate release until one morning when I had been at Putney for about four weeks I was told to report to the Company Commander who advised me that my application had been granted and he intended to make arrangements for me to leave as soon as possible. I was absolutely shattered in view of the very comfortable, well-paid and satisfactory life I was now leading in Putney. I said, 'There must be some mistake, sir, I was told at Bordon that my application had been withdrawn and in any case as I now have a living-out pass and am able to look after my mother every night I would not wish to take advantage of this offer, especially as it would have an adverse effect on my gratuity.'

Whilst it was true that an early release would affect my gratuity, the real reason for my wanting to stay in the Army was that I was now getting good pay for very little work and my mother's larder was being kept well stocked with the best quality food; in fact we had never been able to afford to live as well as we were doing now and I was very reluctant to give that up.

After some discussion I somehow succeeded in convincing the Company Commander that my presence was a real asset to the officers' mess and that I really could not afford to lose any part of my gratuity. Much to my relief he finally agreed to refer the matter back to Brigade Head-quarters with a recommendation that the application be cancelled.

Much to my relief and delight I heard a week later that his recommendation had been accepted and the application was cancelled which meant that the best part of my Army career could continue in the same fantastic manner for several more months until February 1946 when on my twenty-seventh birthday, I received my papers for demobilisation. Because of the marvellous arrangement I had at Putney and as I could not get hold of a forged birth certificate to prove that I was too young to be demobbed, it was with a tinge of sadness and regret that I reported to Olympia for my demobilisation.

This ended the story of my life in the Army which began in the West End of London and ended six and a half years later when I walked out of Olympia with my demob suit and returned home to Fulham.

When I reached the flat, mother was out so I made some tea and sat down and thought what a marvellous feeling it was to be out of the Army and really a free man at last, although I must admit to regretting the loss of the lovely job at Putney.

I recalled some of the experiences I had had since 1939 and came to the conclusion, as I believe most of my generation did, that although Britain had no alternative but to go to war, there had been so many tactical errors and such an awful waste of life. We prayed there would be no need to go to war again.

We certainly had changed from naive young soldiers to hardened veterans and learnt about life and the characteristics of different nationalities.

I thought of some of the brave individuals I had met during the war and whom I felt proud and honoured to have known, for example, the Rifle Brigade major in Calais, Johnny Nicholls who was awarded the VC and the RAF escapee who was shot on the gangway of a Swedish ship. I also remembered some of the characters like Yorkie who was prisoner for the second time, the Lord and his IOUs, and the Yorkshireman who was so proud of his Scottish regiment and his Hogmanay celebrations.

It also came to mind that apart from the German troops in Calais there were others I would have killed at the time if the opportunity had occurred – the Belgian Butcher the dentist (although in hindsight I assume he was doing his best for me), any or all of the Gestapo, Brown Shirts, SS and also any of the Germans responsible for causing so much pain, misery and even death to the inmates of the concentration camps, not forgetting the Camp Commandant who used his bull whip on us, and lastly the WO who insulted us on the ship coming home.

I felt that the initial Army training and discipline enabled me to survive the War and the experiences moulded me into a better, more mature person who respects others and has compassion for all those who are suffering and also a willingness to help others whenever possible. I believe therefore that all the youth of this country should serve in a national service (which would be more concerned with the community rather than military matters) and at the same time to have some discipline instilled in them.

I also sincerely hoped that the politicians succeed in keeping the peace and that any future tyrants were dealt with without any similar catastrophes. Of course my thoughts also turned to my brothers, particularly Ted who was still in the Far East. I wondered when George would get back from Germany now that the War in Europe was over.

My mother returned and interrupted my thoughts on the War and after making fresh tea we began to discuss the future. I arranged to visit John Lewis's to see what sort of job they would offer me, as they were bound to do by law, and after talking with a young personnel officer (who I assumed from his looks and manner was just out of college) he offered me a clerical job at a salary based on a percentage increase in my pre-war salary. I refused it. After a few days searching for something better, I obtained a job with shipping agents in the City of London, and after about eighteen months I joined BOAC.

One lunchtime, I was walking along Bishopsgate when I heard someone shouting, 'Hey, Robbo!' When I looked round I saw a bus conductor waving like mad and recognised Bob Bishop who had been a prisoner in Danzig. Unfortunately the bus never stopped.

That was the only contact I had with anyone I knew in Danzig and I can only assume that despite all our promises to keep in touch, we all became involved with our families and creating a new life that we had not kept in touch. In many ways I regret this so if anyone knows me from the Danzig days that feels as I do and cares to get in touch, I would be delighted to hear from them.

I am now a member of the National Association of Ex-Prisoners of War and I meet other ex-prisoners at the Devon and Cornwall branch which meets at the Royal British Legion Hall in Paignton, Devon. I have not yet met anyone at the meetings who was in the Danzig area. However I shall always feel close to those people and those times, and feel grateful that I survived to get on with the rest of my life.